Assessing Student Achievement in General Education

Edited by Trudy W. Banta

Assessment
UPdate
COLLECTIONS

Copyright © 2007 by John Wiley & Sons, Inc. All rights reserved.

Published by Jossey-Bass
A Wiley Imprint
989 Market Street, San Francisco, CA 94103-1741   www.josseybass.com

Jossey-Bass books and products are available through most bookstores. To contact Jossey-Bass directly call our Customer Care Department within the U.S. at 800-956-7739, outside the U.S. at 317-572-3986, or fax 317-572-4002.

Jossey-Bass also publishes its books in a variety of electronic formats. Some content that appears in print may not be available in electronic books.

Library of Congress Cataloging-in-Publication Data available upon request

Printed in the United States of America
FIRST EDITION
PB Printing   10 9 8 7 6 5 4 3 2 1

Contents

Introduction: Assessing Student Achievement in General Education

Trudy W. Banta

Use of Standardized Tests

For those who followed the work of Secretary of Education Margaret Spellings' Commission on the Future of Higher Education, which issued its report in 2006, the first selection in this issue of **Assessment Update Collections** will bring a profound sense of déja vu. From the outset, commission members considered recommending a national test—or at least state-level testing—for college students focused on communication and analytical reasoning skills. In the first selection here, Sal Corrallo reports that a similar recommendation was considered, and subsequently rejected, in the early 1990s.

The context for considering a national test for college students was actually much fuller in 1990 than in 2006, and the approach to designing the test was more careful and deliberate, involving in each of several stages academics, who ultimately would have to implement the process with students. The stage for a national test was set in 1989, when the National Governors' Association identified six goals for education. The sixth goal stated that by the year 2000 the communication, problem solving, and critical thinking skills of America's college students would increase. The governors' goals were enacted into law in 1993 as Goals 2000.

Of course the only way to tell if skills are increasing is to measure them in some way. So staff at the National Center for Education Statistics (NCES) began in 1991 to explore ways to assess the skills named by the governors. Measurement specialists and other academics with informed perspectives on the assessment of students' learning in college were invited to write papers on the topic of national testing, and these documents were reviewed by others with similar expertise. Authors and reviewers were invited to workshops where the relevant issues were discussed and NCES staff drew conclusions about what should be done next.

NCES staff correctly concluded that a national test would have to be predicated on broad consensus regarding the definitions of communication, problem solving, and critical thinking and appropriate levels of competence for each. Accordingly, grants were awarded to qualified academics to conduct studies aimed at developing the definitions. While these studies yielded good information about the definitions that should underlie a national test for college students, Congressional representatives elected in 1994 concluded that constructing such a test would be too expensive. When Corrallo left NCES in 1996, the six-year effort to find a feasible way to assess college student learning that would yield national averages and permit comparisons across institutions came to an end.

Just as the work of Corrallo and colleagues at NCES between 1990 and 1996 undoubtedly was reviewed by members of the Spellings Commission, Corrallo and associates were influenced to some extent by the findings of research on state-wide testing of college students conducted in states like Tennessee and Washington between 1986 and 1990. In the second selection Robert M. Thorndike describes the studies carried out in the state of Washington in the mid- to late 1980s.

Washington's state Higher Education Coordinating (HEC) board proposed to require statewide testing at the end of the sophomore year. When academic administrators across the state objected to the imposition of a single test on a diverse array of institutions, the HEC board agreed to permit some pilot studies to determine the feasibility of implementing such a mandate. Three tests that were readily available were tried out in community colleges as well as baccalaureate institutions. The studies demonstrated that neither ETS's Academic Profile nor ACT's College Outcome Measures Program (COMP) or Collegiate Assessment of Academic Proficiency (CAAP) was appropriate for the purposes the HEC board staff had in mind. Faculty reviewing the tests did not find them to be valid measures of students' communication, computation, or critical thinking skills. Moreover, the tests were not perceived to be capable of generating information that would be useful in assessing individual student progress or in evaluating curricular effectiveness.

Thorndike's report reveals other objections to the use of standardized tests of generic skills for college students—objections confirmed in studies conducted in other states in the late 1980s and early 1990s. The three standardized tests deployed in Washington were found to assess primarily reading comprehension and, to a lesser extent, computational skills. Moreover, students' scores on the tests revealed high correlations with scores on tests of entering ability (e.g., ACT and SAT scores). Administering the tests at the sophomore level had been assumed to be appropriate since prevailing wisdom held that general education requirements should have been completed by that time. As confirmed in studies conducted in other states, analysis of course-taking patterns in Washington revealed that in fact few students had completed their general education by the end of the second year in college. More damaging still, according to Thorndike, "test scores were found to be negatively correlated with the proportion of general education requirements a student had completed."

Other concerns about standardized testing of generic skills emerged from the Washington studies. In the third selection I have summarized some of these, based on my experience in shepherding the University of Tennessee, Knoxville, response to the state's performance funding initiative. Institutional missions must be considered when comparing test scores across institutions, particularly given that scores on tests of generic skills are highly correlated with measures of entering ability. Valid measures of student achievement must test what faculty in a given context are teaching. Students' motivation to do their best work must be assured if testing of any kind is to be valid. And if students are to take tests seriously, faculty must be convinced of their worth as well.

Faculty on many campuses have taken the time to analyze the content of standardized tests like the CAAP and the College Basic Academic Subjects Exam (CBASE) developed at the University of Missouri and have decided to use them to assess the components of their own general education programs that they find to be covered by the tests. They supplement the standardized tests with other measures to provide more complete coverage of all their primary outcomes. When standardized tests are employed in this fashion—by faculty who have chosen them for their own purposes—faculty engagement in studying and applying the findings in their own classes and departments is ensured and student motivation to do well is much more likely. It is the use of standardized tests to make inferences about educational quality and institutional accountability among institutions with different missions that the studies by Thorndike and others have demonstrated to be problematic.

Use of Locally Designed Instruments

Convinced that standardized tests are not sufficient measures of all that faculty expect college students to learn, faculty across the country have developed their own assessment instruments. In her brief article, Anne G. Scott describes some early steps in this process. First faculty identify the generic skills, such as communication, technical literacy, and global competence, that all students should develop. Then they list specific outcomes associated with each of the skills. By constructing a matrix with courses on one axis and the specific outcomes on the other, faculty can check the outcomes they teach in their courses. A glance at such a matrix will reveal which outcomes are not taught at all and which are taught in so few places that students will not be likely to have sufficient opportunities to practice them. This first set of steps in developing a local approach to assessment will yield information faculty can use immediately to modify curriculum, courses, and instruction without even gathering any information from students.

Assessing Individual Generic Skills

Effective writing is a generic skill that virtually all faculty want students to develop, though the style of expression may vary from discipline to discipline. Consider, for example, the difference between writing about a scientific experiment and building an argument in political science. In one of his *Assessment Measures* columns, Gary R. Pike describes some of the thinking that must form the basis for assessing writing. For instance, will students be given one opportunity to write an essay in a specified amount of time, or will they have several opportunities to draft and refine their product? Will the writing prompt ask students to develop a personal narrative or a persuasive essay? Will scoring be holistic or analytical?

Information literacy is a second broad set of skills that most faculty want students to strengthen while they are in college. My colleague, Howard R. Mzumara, and I describe a process for selecting instruments that may be used to assess information literacy and technological competence. Once again, a prudent first step is to define what campus faculty mean by the concept of information literacy. After that often-difficult discussion has taken place, colleagues can study the components of existing instruments to see if there is a good match with the campus definition or if a locally designed measure is needed.

A third skill that is a stated outcome of most approaches to general education is critical or analytical thinking. Reasoning and problem solving are other terms often linked with critical thinking. In her article, Diane Kelly-Riley recounts the story of a cross-disciplinary campus project that produced a seven-dimension rubric for teaching and assessing critical thinking in every course. Studies have demonstrated that integrating the *Critical Thinking Rubric* in classroom experiences improves critical thinking scores more than is the case when the same instructor teaches the same course without using the rubric.

Moral awareness is a concept not frequently identified as a specific goal of general education. But "a liberal education designed to develop versatile and critical thinkers who can adapt to the professional and ethical challenges they will confront" is important to the faculty who have designed the curriculum at the United States Military Academy, according to James JF Forest and Bruce Keith. In a developmental sequence that takes place throughout the student experience, cadets first learn to recognize moral issues and the ways in which ethics influence decision-making. Then they consider ethical options, counterarguments, and the implications of competing views. In later courses they must analyze cases, identify their moral considerations, and develop morally acceptable responses. Data from multiple sources are used to assess cadets' moral awareness, including a survey of students' confidence in their achievement of the moral awareness goal, students' course products, and employer feedback drawn from focus group interviews of former battalion commanders.

The focus of the faculty-developed assessment approaches discussed to this point has been direct measurement of student performance. Forest and Keith introduce an indirect measure—a student survey in which cadets reflect on their experiences and report their perceptions of the quality of their own learning. Anne Hummer also describes an indirect measure. Dissatisfied with the usual methods—portfolios and performance assessment via video-taping—of measuring multifaceted communication skills, Hummer's colleagues developed the *Student Perception of Communication Skills*. This 50-item questionnaire asks students about self-development of oral and written communication as well as nonverbal and listening skills. Questions also cover peer, faculty, and course contributions to the development of these skills. Hummer's essay addresses the importance of investigating the technical qualities of assessment instruments. She and her colleagues studied the internal consistency and the factor structure of their instrument. Hummer concludes with a detailed summary of the changes faculty made in their teaching based on areas of weakness revealed in students' questionnaire responses.

Valuing diversity is the component of the community college curriculum on which Scott Hunt focuses his selection in this issue. Freshman Experience and Capstone courses provide opportunities for administration of pretest and posttest versions, respectively, of a scenario that gauges students' cultural awareness and appreciation of diversity.

Assessment Methods Applicable Across Knowledge and Skills Areas

We shift our focus now from locally developed assessment approaches that have been applied in specific knowledge and skills areas to generic methods that may be utilized in a variety of these areas. Capstone courses, mentioned here first by Hunt in the previous selection, constitute one such generic approach that is applicable in virtually every discipline. As Terrel L. Rhodes and Susan Agre-Kippenhan note in their article, capstones provide a rich context indeed for administering multiple assessment techniques. In the capstone courses these authors describe, students apply what they have learned in their majors to address community challenges. Student focus groups, reflective essays, end-of-course evaluations, and a post-capstone student survey are some of the ways in which student learning is assessed in these capstones.

Classroom assessment is another effective methodology that can be applied across disciplines. Barbara E. Walvoord, Barbara Bardes, and Janice Denton recount some of the faculty objections to the use of standardized tests that were outlined in previous selections, then tell us how faculty can apply locally developed rubrics to student work in their own classrooms. As these authors note, faculty are much more likely to "close the loop" by using assessment data to improve student learning if they control the process of assessment in their individual classrooms. As faculty uncover student weaknesses and modify their teaching to address these, departmental colleagues can benefit from this information and share some of their own wisdom derived from classroom assessment. Department faculty can share their findings at college and institutional levels. Thus classroom assessment can form the basis for assessing unit and institutional effectiveness as well as the generic skills of individuals.

Phil Speary tells us about a similar classroom-based assessment process adapted for use at a community college. Speary's colleagues assess such skills as critical thinking, speaking, listening, and teamwork in their own courses, using their own assignments. Next they apply a standardized rubric for each skill to their students' classroom products. The new wrinkle here is that Speary's Office of Assessment aggregates data from the rubrics centrally and reports scores to a central committee that can suggest warranted changes in curriculum, instruction, and student services across the institution.

The late Donald W. Farmer was instrumental in establishing outcomes assessment as a distinguishing characteristic of education at King's

College, where "students engage in multiple performance-based assessment experiences in the classroom from the point of entry to the point of graduation." Assessment strategies are embedded in each course and each student has a Competence Growth Plan for eight "transferable skills of liberal learning." Pre- and post-assessments occur in each course, and assessment of the eight transferable skills is the responsibility of each discipline. A unique strategy is the Sophomore-Junior Diagnostic Project that students begin in a sophomore class, carry out over the summer, and present in a junior-level course. Collective consideration of evidence derived from assessment educates faculty about the effectiveness of their work with students. King's faculty also use assessment as a basis for their scholarship. Conference programs and scholarly journals contain a noteworthy number of presentations by King's faculty.

Our final selection, by Philip I. Kramer, reports on an effort in Utah to extend a common approach to assessment across the public institutions in an entire state. In one sense we end this collection where we began—discussing another failed attempt to use a standardized test of generic skills—in this case the Collegiate Assessment of Academic Proficiency (CAAP)—to compare institutions with diverse missions. But in Utah, as in a number of other states, policymakers agreed to authorize a representative group of faculty from various colleges and universities to design their own "content-embedded assessment instruments." The faculty group completed the difficult work of agreeing on nine components of general education that would apply across the system. Then faculty in four disciplines—economics, history, mathematics, and political sciences—developed banks of multiple choice, true-false, and fill-in-the-blank questions for use in a pretest-posttest design intended to measure value added. Faculty were permitted to choose their own items from the banks of test questions. Where the pre- and posttests were applied, students made dramatic gains. But no one was satisfied with the outcomes of the assessment process. Since there was no common test, institutions could not be compared, so policymakers were disappointed. A host of unaddressed methodological issues left faculty wondering how the test results could be used.

The Utah case study demonstrates yet again the enormous set of difficulties we face in attempting to design measures of the learning outcomes associated with general education that will satisfy policy-makers and other stakeholders in higher education. The preponderance of articles selected for this issue demonstrate that at many colleges and universities across the country, faculty are developing course- and curriculum-based measures that enable them to detect strengths and weaknesses in the learning of groups of students. This evidence is being used to improve courses, curricula, and student services. But in developing the measures that our stakeholders envision for the purpose of comparing the quality and accountability of various institutions, we have made very little progress in the two decades since Robert Thorndike conducted his studies in the mid-1980s.

Use of Standardized Tests

The National Assessment of College Student Learning: Current and Future Activities

Sal Corrallo

Look for: A chronicle of the activities directed at developing a national test for college students that were undertaken by staff of the National Center for Education Statistics (NCES) between 1990 and 1996. While the NCES approach was deliberate and careful, the effort to develop a national test was ultimately judged too costly to pursue. From Assessment Update 8:4 (1996).

The National Education Goals were first developed by the nation's governors in 1989. They identified a set of aspirations for enhancing the quality of education at all levels in order to ensure that the nation's work force would have the skills to compete in world markets in the twenty-first century. The National Education Goals were later enacted into law in 1993 under the Goals 2000 legislation. In direct response to the adoption of the goals, the National Center for Education Statistics (NCES) of the U.S. Department of Education has, since 1991, had an active program of exploring ways to assess the set of skills needed by college graduates identified under Goal 6, Objective 5. Higher-order communication, problem solving, and critical thinking skills are on this list. Planning workshops were conducted in 1991 to identify issues and concerns and, in 1992, to identify the steps necessary to begin the process of defining the skills. Both series of workshops produced working papers that were later published and distributed to the higher education community.

In 1993, NCES prepared a request for proposals (REP) to obtain a consensus on the skills, and appropriate levels of competence for each, needed by college graduates. The results were to be used as a basis for a national assessment of college student learning. The RFP was not funded due to budget constraints. Furthermore, it was clear that NCES would not soon have sufficient resources to conduct the comprehensive national study originally envisaged. This situation required implementation of an alternative strategy.

Over the next three years, from 1994 to 1996, NCES funded a scaled-down effort to identify the core skills needed by college graduates in the workplace. The National Center for Postsecondary Teaching, Learning, and Assessment (NCPTLA) at Pennsylvania State University used a two-stage Delphi panel to define five skill areas: speaking and listening, writing, critical thinking, reading, and problem solving. Each skill panel was composed of 200 members drawn from the academic and business communities. The first report, covering the first three skill areas, was published in July 1995 (Jones and others, 1995). The results from the final two panels, reading and problem solving, will be completed late in 1996. These reports will provide the initial listing of skills needed by college graduates as cited in the Goals 2000 legislation. However, they do not indicate the expected levels of competence for specific work or citizenship activities.

Concurrent with the NCPTLA studies, NCES, in cooperation with the Department of Labor (DOL), set out to define a generic set of job skills in high-performance workplace settings. This activity was designed as a follow-up to the DOL Secretary's Commission on Achieving Necessary Skills (SCANS) project through the National Job Analysis Study. (SCANS was convened in 1990 to determine the skills American workers need for job success in a global market and to create an action plan for the development of those skills.) Findings will concern specific tasks and related skills utilized by a national sample of workers across professions in high-performance workplace settings. The survey of job-specific tasks and related skills stands in contrast to the judgmental approach used in the NCPTLA Goals 2000 skills study. Although the original intent of the DOL study was to focus on the skills needed by high school graduates, this study is expected to identify sets of skills for the larger workforce, including college graduates. Once the generic skills have been identified, appropriate assessment instruments are to be developed that can be used in a new or ongoing study. A final report is not expected before the end of 1996.

NCES also has turned its attention toward state-level assessment efforts as a potential source of information on student learning. A 1995 American College Testing survey of postsecondary assessment needs at the state and institutional levels indicated that many of the skills specified in the National Education Goals are being assessed, although unevenly (Steele, 1996). To gain further insights on the potential use of current state efforts as a proxy for a national assessment, NCES conducted a third planning conference in December 1995. Directors of postsecondary assessment from all 50 states and selected territories were invited to attend. The agenda focused on (1) identification of the knowledge and skills being assessed at the state level and how they relate to the skills identified in the National Education Goals; (2) the frequency, reliability, consistency, and compatibility of the information collected across the states; and (3) activities that can help states broaden and enhance their assessment programs. Workshop participants surveyed in advance by Peter Ewell indicated that current state efforts are far less comprehensive than might be expected (Ewell, 1996). About 80% of the states have formal assessment programs. This is essentially unchanged from a 1989 survey conducted by Ewell, Finney, and Lenth (1990). According to Ewell, half of the states with such programs use an institution-based approach as opposed to statewide assessment. Few states, whether institution- or state-based in their assessment efforts, use common measures. One reason for the diversity in assessment approaches is that each state, and each institution within the state, has unique educational priorities. The assessment approaches and outcomes reflect those differences.

Ewell (1996) suggested that since 1989 states have shifted their emphasis from use of assessment for program improvement to use for accountability purposes. He believes this may make it more difficult to build campus support for the development of indicators of student learning.

As a side note, Ewell observed that it is often easier to reach agreement on assessment goals and instruments within a state if there is a national or regional push for assessment. This influence might be exerted through regional accreditation agencies, professional associations, or the federal government. In support of this argument are the experiences of the National Assessment of Educational Progress (NAEP) (see White, 1994) and the National Adult Literacy Survey (NALS) (see Kirsch, Jungeblut, Jenkins, and Kolstad, 1993). Designers of both surveys had to identify and define levels of achievement for skills they ultimately assessed. In addition to the national study, survey populations for both NAEP and NALS were enhanced as a number of states opted to contract with NCES to provide state-level assessments of learning.

Nonetheless, based on current activities and plans, it seems clear that no assessment of the skills college graduates bring to the workplace and to the practice of citizenship will occur through casual or volunteer efforts at the institution or state level. The current budget climate at the national level makes it unlikely that a new national assessment of college student learning can be launched.

However, several NCES surveys are candidates for assessing college student learning. The 1993 National Adult Literacy Survey measured prose, document, and quantitative literacy on a scale developed by staff of the Educational Testing Service. The NALS results revealed that roughly one in six college graduates scored in the lowest two of five literacy levels, a rather discouraging finding. Future surveys of adult literacy might be broadened to include the workplace and citizenship skills needed by college graduates.

Another potential source of information is an NCES survey of college graduates conducted by telephone. This might be broadened to add an employer component to determine how well recent college graduates are prepared for the work experience. Although there would be no direct assessment of skills, such data would provide much the same type of information as is often used to set standards for hiring, that is, informed judgment based on experience on the job. With appropriate enlargement of the sample, results can be reported by course of study, type of institution, and state.

The final, and perhaps the most desirable, alternative is to extend NAEP to the end of the second year of college. The National Job Analysis Study will ultimately provide a set of test items that can be used to determine levels of attainment for a generic set of workplace skills. Consideration might also be given to using these or similar items from the Grade 12 form of NAEP so that comparisons can be made with the college-level NAEP. It might also be desirable to move the twelfth-grade NAEP back to the eleventh grade, focusing the testing around the workplace skills and content areas identified in National Goal 3.2, that is, communication and thinking skills in addition to science and mathematics. This approach might be more valuable to students and schools and would give the schools time to help students make up deficiencies in the twelfth year.

Which approach, if any, will be considered is an open question. However, unless renewed effort by the nation's governors rekindles interest in the National Education Goals, it is likely that the project at the national level will be put on hold for the immediate future. If anything is to happen, it will only be through increased state interest and effort. If such effort occurs, it should begin with a concern for improving teaching and learning of the skills and knowledge college graduates need after they graduate. The end result should be assessment that ensures that students possess and can use skills and knowledge they will need to lead successful and productive lives.

References

Ewell, P. T. "The Current Pattern of State-Level Assessment: Results of a National Inventory." *Assessment Update*, 1996, *8*(3), 1–2, 12–13, 15.

Ewell, P. T., Finney, J., and Lenth, C. "Filling in the Mosaic: The Emerging Pattern of State-Based Assessment." *AAHE Bulletin*, 1990, *43*(8).

Jones, E. A., Hoffman, S., Moore, L. M., Radcliff, G., Tibbetts, S., Click, B. A. L., III, National Center on Postsecondary Teaching, Learning, and Assessment, The Pennsylvania State University. *National Assessment of College Student Learning: Identifying College Graduates' Essential Skills in Writing, Speech, Listening, and Critical Thinking*. Washington, DC: National Center for Education Statistics, 1995.

Kirsch, I. S., Jungeblut, A., Jenkins, L., and Kolstad, A. *Adult Literacy in America.* Washington, D.C.: National Center for Education Statistics, 1993.

Steele, J. M. "Postsecondary Assessment Needs: Implications for State Policy." *Assessment Update*, 1996, 8(2), 1–2, 12–13, 15.

White, S. *Overview of NAEP Assessment Frameworks.* Washington, DC: National Center for Education Statistics, 1994.

In 1996, Sal Corrallo was a former senior staff member at the National Center for Education Statistics, U.S. Department of Education.

The Washington State Assessment Experience

Robert M. Thorndike

Look for: Results of pilot studies conducted in Washington in the 1980s for the purpose of evaluating the use of three standardized instruments in assessing the progress of individual students and curricular success. Faculty representing 2- and 4-year institutions across the state concluded that none of the tests were valid for either purpose. From Assessment Update *2:2 (1990).*

The legislature and Higher Education Coordinating (HEC) board of Washington State became increasingly aware of the issue of outcomes assessment during the latter half of the 1980s. As part of its long-range master plan for academic excellence, the HEC board proposed to require statewide administration of a test to assess academic skills at the end of the sophomore year, a point that the board assumed corresponded closely to completion of the general education portion of a student's college career.

The provosts of the state's six baccalaureate institutions and the governing board of the community college system raised objections to the imposition of a single test to be applied to all students because of the wide diversity in student bodies and institutional missions. They also objected to the assumption that there was a time at which it was appropriate to test all students for the acquisition of these skills. As a compromise, the HEC board agreed to let the institutions carry out pilot studies to determine whether such a testing program was feasible and could yield information useful to academic decision making.

Two pilot studies were carried out in parallel and in cooperation by the community college system and by the baccalaureate institutions to maximize the interinstitutional applicability of the results. Both studies evaluated the objective test of the College Outcome Measures Program (COMP), and pilot versions of the Collegiate Assessment of Academic Proficiency (CAAP) and the Academic Profile. The primary conclusion of these pilot studies was that none of the tests examined were appropriate for the purposes specified in the HEC board master plan. Specifically, the master plan called for the assessment of skills in communication, computation, and critical thinking. Analysis of test content by faculty committees at each institution revealed that the faculty did not perceive the tests to be valid measures of these skills. Furthermore, the faculty did not see results obtained from the tests as likely to give information useful in evaluating either the progress of individual students or the success of the curriculum.

The tests were administered to over 1,300 students near the end of their sophomore year. Analysis of student responses showed that the tests measured primarily reading comprehension and, to a lesser extent, computational ability. Scores correlated highly with performance on college entrance tests and therefore added little to what was already known about student ability. Analysis of student course-taking patterns revealed that relatively few students, particularly at baccalaureate institutions, completed their general education requirements during the first two years, thus making it impossible to draw conclusions about the effectiveness of such programs. In addition, test scores were found to be negatively correlated with the proportion of general education requirements a student had completed.

Upon receipt of the report of the pilot study, the members of the HEC board called on each institution to define and develop methods for assessing the achievement of its own objectives, as well as the following elements: student entry characteristics; achievement in communication and computation skills by midpoint in the academic career; achievement in the major at the conclusion of the college career; detailed internal and external review of program objectives, requirements, and facilities; surveys of alumni attitudes toward their education; and surveys of employer satisfaction with the institution's graduates.

In addition, institutions were asked to prepare proposals for assessing other student characteristics that might be appropriate in light of their institutional missions and to maintain close cooperation and communication with each other. The legislature appropriated $2.8 million in the 1989–91 biennium for assessment activities.

A principle guiding all attempts to assess student cognitive skills in the state is the importance of student motivation. Conducting the pilot study made it clear to all concerned that measures to ensure a high and relatively uniform level of motivation among the students being assessed is absolutely essential to obtaining meaningful and useful results. Students must have a stake in the outcomes of assessment, either by believing in the efficacy of the procedure and its ownership by students, or in terms of the level of performance having personal consequences.

For the present, both the institutions and state policymakers have rejected making students' advancement in the educational program contingent on achieving a particular score on a common exam or other standard performance measure. The solution to the motivation problem that has been adopted for trial use throughout the state is for each institution to embed measures of achievement that transcend individual courses into as many aspects of the normal curriculum as possible. Ways to expand the emphasis on writing throughout the curriculum are being explored, as are ways to spread the responsibility for evaluation of that writing across the faculty. Departments are being encouraged to develop or expand capstone experiences, such as integrative courses and senior theses, as part of the normal curriculum for every student. The results of such experiences can be evaluated by faculty from different departments or institutions to provide the needed external validation of performance standards.

Several institutions are working on problems related to the analysis of writing portfolios. In addition, each institution is developing interviews or questionnaires to tap student, alumni, and employer perceptions and each is preparing to feed information from these sources into the institutional decision-making process. The community college system has decided to collect detailed information on placement outcomes from students in their vocational programs and on the success of transfer students in their academic programs.

The legislature and HEC board have made it clear that the institutions must report how assessment results are being used to improve instruction. But state authorities have recognized the diversity among the institutions as a strength and have reaffirmed institutional autonomy over the details of their assessment initiatives. The climate for assessment generally is positive across the state, and many faculty and administrators are looking forward to the chance to develop and use objective information to promote self-examination and constructive change. The movement that many faculty and administrators viewed with alarm a year ago has come to be seen as an opportunity.

In 1990, Robert M. Thorndike was professor of psychology at Western Washington University.

Reliving the History of Large-Scale Assessment in Higher Education

Trudy W. Banta

Look for: A reasoned argument against the use of standardized tests for college students in making judgments about institutional quality. The points summarized here are based on research conducted by the author and colleagues as they administered standardized tests to thousands of freshmen and seniors at the University of Tennessee in response to the performance funding initiative of the Tennessee Higher Education commission. From Assessment Update 18:4 (2006).

In 1986, Gary Pike and I joined forces to guide the University of Tennessee, Knoxville's response to the Tennessee Higher Education Commission's (THEC) performance funding initiative. Our experience in administering the ACT College Outcome Measures Project (COMP) exam, which was THEC's required measure of student learning and general education at that time, meant that we had a particularly well informed perspective on national testing when in 1990 the U.S. Department of Education (DOE) began to seek advice about developing a standardized test for college students. I wrote one of the fifteen papers on that topic that were commissioned by the DOE, and in 1991 and 1992, Gary and I found ourselves speaking at several national meetings and writing journal articles about the use of tests in higher education and about value-added assessment in particular. On the basis of our analyses of freshman and senior COMP scores, we had found gain scores to be remarkably unreliable, and we felt compelled to share that knowledge whenever an audience would listen.

Despite the best efforts of scholars and practitioners to dissuade the powers in Washington, the DOE was negotiating with the Educational Testing Service (ETS) to develop a national test when the 1994 congressional election swept fiscal conservatives into office. The new congress decided that the nation could not afford to develop a national test at that time. Could congressional elections in 2006 win a similar reprieve for higher education? This is not as likely at this point in our history. In September, the Commission on the Future of Higher Education will issue its report, and while the commission may not recommend a national test, it probably will provide strong encouragement for states to extend the now-familiar concept of achievement testing for high school students to the college level. Moreover, a number of national higher education associations have appointed their own commissions to consider ways to try to quench the thirst of political and governmental stakeholders for some simple, readily understood measures of accountability for colleges and universities.

Let me state the obvious at the outset: I am not arguing against assessment of student learning! I have devoted much of my career to helping faculty find measures of learning that make sense in a given context. But the issue of context is huge. A major strength of American higher education is its diversity. We have religiously affiliated colleges, same-sex institutions, technical universities, and campuses where problem-based learning is emphasized. No single test can incorporate content that will enable students at all these kinds of institutions to demonstrate the particular strengths they have developed during their college experiences.

While the road has proven to be long and full of potholes, I still have high hopes that student electronic portfolios—the most authentic and comprehensive measurement system available to us—can give us the simple, readily understood measures of student learning that external stakeholders crave. But standing between us and that goal are the following milestones: (1) faculty must agree on some general student learning outcomes, then operationalize them in rubrics that can be applied to student work across a variety of disparate disciplines; (2) information technology experts must design systems that will make it possible for thousands of students to create electronic archives containing millions of artifacts that can be evaluated against the rubrics, then aggregated for easy reporting (for example, 68 percent of the seniors in geography at IUPUI can think critically, which is operationally defined as follows . . .); (3) students must be required to place artifacts in their portfolios over their entire academic careers so that we can assess development and, thus, value added; (4) students must be motivated to take the development of their portfolios seriously, which means that even though the artifacts in the portfolios may have been graded previously by a course instructor, we also need to find the time to assess the contents of the portfolios and judge them satisfactory or unsatisfactory using the rubrics developed in item (1) above.

While we await the development of the perfect portfolio system—that is, a form considered valid by faculty, students, and external stakeholders, there are many other measures that suit individual contexts. Licensing and certification exams are considered valid measures by faculty and employers in professional fields like medicine, nursing, and law. Senior projects assessed by employers in a given field provide convincing evidence of student learning, as do clinical internships for dental students and student teaching for future teachers. When evidence from such culminating experiences for seniors is combined with employer ratings of competence on the job for graduates in a given discipline, a powerful story indeed can be assembled for purposes of external reporting.

Gary Pike (2006) provides an elegant statistical analysis of some of the concerns we have about one particular measure of college student learning that is currently being touted by some of our stakeholders. Let me add some practical concerns of my own about mandated large-scale standardized testing with high stakes. These concerns follow from my earlier outline of the steps we need to take to make valid assessment tools of student electronic portfolios.

In his 1999 Angoff lecture at ETS, James Pelligrino (2004) asserted, "Assessment that is external to an on-going process of learning and teaching . . . will not produce the desired outcomes by itself. . . . Assessment must become an essential part of the design and enactment of contemporary learning environments" (p. 5). Any valid measure of student achievement must do a reasonable job of testing what faculty in a given context are trying to teach. This presupposes that the faculty in a major (or in an institution or in a state) can agree on definitions of what they want students to learn—a substantial achievement in itself. Giving a test like the Collegiate Learning Assessment (CLA) can serve as an interesting point of departure for faculty discussion about the kind and quality of learning they seek in their students. But there is no possibility that a single instrument given in a period of a few hours can provide a valid measure of the kinds of critical thinking or even the kinds of writing that faculty in engineering, history, and art, for example, expect their students to develop.

On any given test, students majoring in some disciplines will be advantaged, while others will be disadvantaged. Gary and I learned, for instance, that having the only architecture school in a public institution in Tennessee gave the University of Tennessee, Knoxville, a decided advantage on the COMP exam (an instrument that is no longer offered by ACT). One set of questions on the COMP exam was based on the student's ability to calculate the area of a room. Our architecture majors inevitably achieved near-perfect scores on that section, and in some years, that one fact was enough to send our scores above the averages required for performance funding for total score and for gain (value added).

A test that requires students to do a lot of reading will likely advantage literature majors and disadvantage visual communication majors because these two groups spend their learning time in college in very different ways. No standardized exam is truly content-free, and if it were, it would be a better test of general intelligence than of what is learned in college. The near-perfect correlation of CLA scores with ACT and SAT scores suggests that the CLA may be a better measure of the abilities students bring with them than of the learning they acquire in college.

We know from our experience of at least twenty-five years that (1) most college students will not even make the effort to take a test that is not required and (2) even if a test is required, students may not give it their best effort unless their performance has some consequences. If faculty are not convinced that a test yields scores that tell them something important about their students, their students will not consider the test important, either. While a prize or other recognition for high scores might motivate some students to strive for their best performance, what will motivate those who feel they have no chance to achieve a high score to give the test more than minimal effort? And for students who fail to achieve a set minimum score, what will be the consequences? Will they be told they can't graduate? Will they have to retake courses in which they have A, B, or C grades or take new courses in areas in which their test scores suggest they have deficits? If coursework is required, who will have to pay for it—the student or the institution that presumably failed to help them learn what the test said they needed to know?

It is not defensible to infer that differences in standardized test scores reflect differences in the quality of education offered at different colleges and universities, because it is individual differences among the students taking the test that account for most of these differences—and in ways we don't yet understand very well (Pike, 2006). Individual student differences influence the college choices that students make in the first place. An affluent eighteen-year-old can travel to any campus in the country and can afford to spend four years there and graduate in four years. A thirty-two- year-old working in a city may decide to enter an urban university close to home, enjoy courses—some of which are online—from three other institutions, and take ten years to graduate. The first student (A) has grown up surrounded by books and computers and parents who began talking about what college A might attend before A could walk. The second student (B) has parents who worked in manufacturing jobs and never considered going to college; the daily newspaper and television provided the intellectual stimulation for B as he grew up. Both A and B decide to major in history. But A spends lots of time in a rare book collection studying medieval manuscripts, while B focuses on public history and local museums provide the principal sites for his learning. A spends full time on her studies. B works over thirty hours per week and lives at home, where his parents think college involves just going to class, resent any time he spends studying, and criticize B for not working full time.

The selective private college A chooses and the urban public university B attends meet the needs of those two different individuals for higher education. But the two institutions vary enormously in terms of the levels of preparedness of the students they attract; the kinds of sustained learning experiences their students can afford (full-time student A can consider study-abroad options, while part-time student B is place-bound, for example); the proportion of credits that students transfer from other institutions; the mix of majors they provide; and the range of faculty expertise that students encounter within each major, just to name a few important differences. Yet both institutions have a few graduates who become company presidents, some who become excellent parents, and a few who end up as convicted felons. Why? What it is about these two institutions that contributes to these outcomes? This is the information we really need from instruments that purport to assess collegiate learning. Unfortunately, today's state-of-the-art standardized tests will not give us this information, in large part because we cannot tease out the differential effects of college from the individual human differences that distinguish college students from each other.

Clearly, we must confront the current press to assess with a test. We need to train the focus of our most distinguished measurement experts on finding reliable, valid measures of generic skills, disciplinary knowledge and skills, performance (application of skills), and the value added by a college education. But we cannot afford to place all our bets on the most promising three-year-old horse out of the starting gate, expecting a simple ride to victory. We have over twenty-five years of experience with these animals called standardized tests, and they haven't given us a win with the public yet. Those who ignore this history will be condemned to relive it.

References

Pelligrino, J. W. (2004). *The Evolution of Educational Assessment: Considering the Past and Imagining the Future*. Princeton, NJ: Policy Evaluation and Research Center, Educational Testing Service.

Pike, G. R. (2006). "Value-Added Models and the Collegiate Learning Assessment." *Assessment Update*, 2006, *18*(4), 5–7.

In 2006, Trudy W. Banta was vice chancellor for planning and institutional improvement at Indiana University Purdue-University Indianapolis.

Use of Locally Designed Instruments

The Role of Assessment in Linking Faculty Teaching to Student Outcomes

Anne G. Scott

Look for: Development of a skills X courses matrix that can help faculty spot course and curricular gaps. From Assessment Update 11:1 (1999).

The Arizona International Campus (AIC) of the University of Arizona has implemented a curriculum that is both interdisciplinary and focused on specific skills, competencies, and substantive knowledge as student outcomes. The skills and competencies targeted by AIC are communication, problem solving, quantitative and qualitative analysis, technical literacy, moral discernment, and global and intercultural competence. These skills and competencies are not identified with particular courses on campus but are integrated throughout the curriculum.

The assessment approach designed by the faculty in consultation with the assessment office is to create checklists for each of the skills and competencies. The checklists contain the specific outcomes for each of the skills and competencies. They are distributed to faculty members teaching required core courses. These faculty are asked to mark the skills they teach and to provide the course name, and to mark skills they do not teach but are interested in learning more about in order to incorporate the skills into their instruction. When feedback from all faculty is collated, gaps appear. For example, in the case of technology, it is evident that faculty sufficiently cover word processing, spreadsheet, and Internet functions. But certain areas are not covered at all. Even worse, databases are not covered and no one is even interested in doing this.

One benefit of this procedure is that faculty become more interested and involved in assessment as they reevaluate their own teaching repertoire. Also, by tying the faculty reward system to student outcomes it is possible to close the gaps through positive action. Last summer several faculty attended a technology workshop to learn how to incorporate the latest computer technology into their classrooms. They were encouraged (and rewarded) not only for incorporating what they learned into their teaching but also for sharing that knowledge with other faculty members.

In 1999, Anne G. Scott was director of institutional research, evaluation, and assessment at Arizona International College of the University of Arizona.

Assessing Individual Generic Skills

Assessment Measures

Gary R. Pike

Look for: Some basic questions that must be addressed in developing writing assessments. For example, will the writing prompt ask students to develop a personal narrative or a persuasive essay? Will holistic or analytical scoring be used? From Assessment Update 5:5 *(1993).*

Since coming to the Center for Educational Assessment (CEA) in January, one of my major projects has been the statewide assessment of student writing for grades K–12. Because many colleges and universities are interested in assessing the quality of student writing as part of their evaluation of general education programs (or their writing-across-the-curriculum programs), I thought that it might be helpful to recount some of our experiences. In this column I will provide a brief description of the writing assessment program in Missouri and discuss some of the basic questions that must be addressed in developing a writing assessment program. In a subsequent column, I will be discussing some of the findings of recent CEA evaluations of the Missouri Writing Assessment program.

The easiest way to organize this description is to examine three of the key questions that should be answered in order to establish a viable writing assessment program. I want to stress that there are no "right" answers to these questions. However, the ways in which institutions answer them profoundly shape the nature of writing assessment on their campuses.

The first question is "What sort of writing task should be used?" The choice initially is between what I call a one-shot writing assessment and an assessment of the process of writing. In the one-shot assessment, students are given a topic and told that they have a certain amount of time (usually about one hour) to write an essay. This approach is frequently used in commercial general education assessment instruments, such as the Academic Profile and College BASE. The strength of the one-shot method is its ease of administration. Its limitation is that it usually does not reflect the writing process students use.

The alternative, a process-writing approach, is designed to parallel more closely the actual writing process of students. The present Missouri Writing Assessment is an example of the process-writing approach. Students are allotted three class periods in which to write. The first is devoted to prewriting activities and an initial draft. During the second class period, students are encouraged to continue drafting and to begin revising their essays. During the final period, students complete their revisions and prepare a final copy of the essay.

Clearly, the major liability of the process-writing approach is the time required for administration and scoring. Scoring takes longer because the essays tend to be longer. However, the time is well spent. Research conducted by CEA has found that the process-writing approach has much greater face validity with classroom teachers than the one-shot approach. In addition, scores tend to be somewhat higher, and there is greater variability in scores. When a one-shot writing assessment was used in Missouri, it was discovered that 85% of the students received a score of 3 on a six-point scale. With the process-writing approach, slightly less than 40% of the students received a score of 3.

Once the nature of the task has been defined, assessment professionals are confronted with the choice of which type of writing prompt to use (for example, personal narrative, expository essay, or persuasive essay). This choice is not trivial. Several researchers have reported that writing scores vary more across types of writing than across students. In 1992, most students in Missouri wrote expository essays. However, a randomly selected subsample of students wrote personal narratives. Results indicated that students who wrote personal narratives had significantly higher scores than students who wrote expository essays (half a point higher on a six-point scale).

A related issue in selecting writing prompts is whether the topics should be generic or discipline specific. Recently, I have been working with several community colleges that are developing assessment programs. One is implementing writing assessment. In pilot testing the writing assessment, it was discovered that standards for writing were significantly different across the disciplines (sciences, social sciences, humanities, and so on). If institutions elect to use a generic writing prompt, they run the risk of not assessing the kinds of writing performance expected of their students. On the other hand, if an institution administers many different kinds of writing prompts, it may be difficult or impossible to generalize across writing samples and arrive at an overall evaluation of the general education writing program.

Irrespective of the type of prompt selected, the directions should include sufficient introductory material to provide the students with a context for the writing exercise. At a minimum, students need to know the purpose for the essay and the intended audience.

The final question that must be answered in developing a writing assessment concerns the type of scoring rubric to be used. For simplicity I will focus on the choice between holistic and analytical rubrics. Holistic rubrics require raters to make a global evaluation of writing samples based on the assumption that the overall impression conveyed by an essay is greater than the sum of its parts. Analytical scoring rubrics contain multiple scoring scales covering different aspects of writing, such as ideas and content, organization, word choice, sentence structure, voice, and so forth. Many of the final recommendations suggest that holistic approaches be used for summative end-of-term assessment and that analytical approaches be used for formative assessment designed to provide feedback to students.

Despite the ongoing debate over the relative merits of holistic and analytical scoring methods, one fact is clear. Analytical scoring methods are substantially more time-consuming than holistic ones. For example, one study found that it took 2 times as long to train raters and score essays using analytical methods. At the present time, CEA and the Missouri Department of Elementary and Secondary Education are conducting a study comparing holistic and analytical scoring approaches. The results of that research will be included in a subsequent column on writing assessment.

In 1993, Gary R. Pike was senior research analyst for the Center for Educational Assessment at the University of Missouri, Columbia.

Assessing Information Literacy and Technological Competence

Trudy W. Banta, Howard R. Mzumara

Look for: An approach to selecting an instrument to assess a generic skill as conceptualized on a given campus. Information literacy is the skill on which this study is focused. From Assessment Update 16:5 (2004).

Essential skills for college students and graduates in the twenty-first century include the abilities to use technology to search for and locate information relevant to a particular question or problem, then to make judgments about the credibility and usefulness of the information, and finally to apply the information appropriately to answer the given question or solve the problem. Faculty on most campuses are discussing ways to teach and assess these skills, and our institution, Indiana University-Purdue University Indianapolis (IUPUI), is no exception.

Defining Information Literacy

A first step is to define information literacy. Fortunately, we have some good models to shape our initial thinking. For instance, the Association of College and Research Libraries (ACRL) has defined information literacy as "a set of abilities requiring individuals to recognize when information is needed . . . [then] locate, evaluate, and use effectively the needed information" (2000, n.p.). The ACRL has described seven components of information literacy:

1. Recognize and define the need for information
2. Initiate a search strategy
3. Locate information in multiple sources
4. Determine the usefulness of the information
5. Interpret and use the information
6. Communicate the findings of the information-seeking process
7. Evaluate the product and the process, determining how well the final product met the information need and whether the steps taken in the process were appropriate and efficient

Some institutions have chosen to distinguish information literacy from one of its component skills, competence in using information technology. The Association of College and Research Libraries (2000) defines information technology skills as those associated with an individual's use of computers, software applications, databases, and other technologies to achieve an academic, work-related, or personal goal.

At IUPUI, the campus approach to general education is based on six learning outcomes called principles of undergraduate learning (PULs) that were adopted by our Faculty Council in 1998. The PULs are (1) core communication and quantitative skills; (2) critical thinking; (3) integration and application of knowledge; (4) intellectual depth, breadth, and adaptiveness; (5) understanding society and culture; and (6) values and ethics. (For a fuller description of the PULs, consult <ww.iport.iupui.edu/teach/teach_pul.htm>) Information literacy and information technology skills are considered components of PUL #1, core communication and quantitative skills.

In 2002, the campuswide, faculty-led Program Review and Assessment Committee at IUPUI named ten subcommittees and charged each with the responsibility of defining for a particular PUL introductory and intermediate levels of competence and means of assessing student learning at each of these levels. PUL #1 required four subcommittees, one for each of its components: writing, listening and speaking, quantitative reasoning, and information literacy. Introductory competence was defined for the subcommittees as the level of knowledge and skills IUPUI students will be expected to demonstrate on completion of twenty-six credit hours; intermediate competence will be demonstrated on completion of fifty-six credit hours.

Members of the subcommittee with responsibility for information literacy reviewed pertinent literature that had been developed with ALA and ACRL resources, as well as documents from other sources. They quickly decided to include the two areas of information literacy and information technology in their skills definition. Then they began the task of describing introductory and intermediate levels of competence, where and how these skills would be taught and learned, and how competence might be demonstrated and assessed. As an example, one area of competence is focused on organization and use of information. The introductory level is defined as follows: "Student organizes and uses information effectively to accomplish a specific purpose." Such skills can be taught and learned through writing assignments and oral presentations across the disciplines. A student might demonstrate competence at this level by identifying the information sources used in an assignment and citing these sources appropriately. At an intermediate level, the student should demonstrate an understanding that a variety of sources will provide additional evidence on a topic; students will learn this skill through work on research papers and independent research projects.

Selecting Assessment Tools

Once the subcommittee had defined levels of competence, methods for teaching and learning, and types of evidence that might be used to demonstrate information literacy and information technology skills and knowledge, the next step was to review existing assessment instruments to see whether they provided opportunities for students to demonstrate that they had acquired the specified knowledge and skills.

Subcommittee members quickly discovered a variety of homegrown online tutorial systems designed by faculty and staff at other universities, including Cornell University <http://www.library.cornell.edu/olinuris/ref/research/tutorial.html>, Griffith University <http://www.griffith. edu.au/ins/training/library/home_lrt.html>, Purdue University <http:// core.lib.purdue.edu/>, and the University of Texas System <http://tilt. lib.utsystem.edu/>. Most of these tutorial systems not only assist students in developing skills but also incorporate online testing modules. Of the university-based systems, the one developed at James Madison University <http://www.lib.jmu.edu/library/gold/ modules.htm> most impressed the reviewers because reliability and validity issues are addressed in the literature about this system.

Members of the subcommittee chose to focus most attention, however, on four assessment systems that are supported by commercial vendors. These include tools developed by Tek.Xam <www.tekxam .com>, NETg <www.netg.com>, Smart- Force (SkillSoft) <www.skillsoft.com>, and Microsoft Office User Specialist <www.microsoft.com/traincert/ mcp/officespecialist/requirements.asp>. Subcommittee members compared the four systems on five dimensions: (1) primary function: training, certification, or testing; (2) content or skill areas addressed; (3) special design features, such as levels of competence addressed and opportunities for customization and tracking of progress for individuals and groups; (4) mode of administration—in a proctored or unproctored environment; and (5) cost.

A primary consideration for subcommittee members in making the decision to recommend one or more information literacy assessment tools was the degree of alignment between the content presented and tested by each system and the content specified in the introductory and intermediate competence statements developed by the subcommittee. When this criterion was applied, it is not surprising that one of the recommendations was for IUPUI faculty to develop their own assessment tools to match the learning outcomes they seek.

The choice among the four assessment systems offered by commercial vendors also was based on idiosyncrasies that obtain within Indiana University. As a result of prior arrangements, NETg courses and related tests are available online at no cost to IUPUI faculty, staff, and students. The fact that this system is already available for teaching and testing at no additional cost to the institution addressed both the issues of alignment with current content and cost.

Implications of the IUPUI Initiative

The specific recommendations that emanated from the Subcommittee on Information Literacy and Information Technology at IUPUI are not as important as the details of the process in which subcommittee members engaged. First, they reviewed a body of literature that already is quite helpful and is getting better every day. Guided by the definitions and standards derived from the literature, subcommittee members developed specific definitions for introductory and intermediate levels of competence in information literacy and information technology, indicated how associated knowledge and skills might be taught and learned, then described the kinds of evidence that students could use to demonstrate competence at a given level.

Next, subcommittee members reviewed existing systems for delivering both training and assessment, looking for the best match between the learning outcomes described by IUPUI faculty and the content defined by the system vendors. Other factors, especially cost, also were considered in the decision about which assessment system to recommend for campus use. This decision might turn out quite differently on another campus, where different definitions of competence in information literacy will have been developed. But the process we have described has widespread applicability.

Reference

Association of College and Research Libraries. "Information Literacy Competency Standards for Higher Education: Standards, Performance Indicators, and Outcomes." [http://www.ala.org/ala/acrl/acrlstandards/informationliteracycompetency.htm]. Jan. 2000.

In 2004, Trudy W. Banta was vice chancellor for planning and institutional improvement, and Howard R. Mzumara was director of the Testing Center and chair of the Subcommittee on Information Literacy and Information Technology at Indiana University-Purdue University Indianapolis.

Washington State University Critical Thinking Project: Improving Student Learning Outcomes through Faculty Practice

Diane Kelly-Riley

Look for: Faculty collaboration across disciplines to develop a critical thinking rubric that can be used as an instructional guide as well as an evaluation tool. Studies have demonstrated that use of the rubric can produce score gains in critical thinking. From Assessment Update *15:4 (2003).*

When Washington Sate University (WSU) began general education reform in the late 1980s, the faculty proposed to achieve learning goals through general education curriculum and writing-across-the-curriculum initiatives. While we fully integrated writing into all aspects of our undergraduate curriculum, particularly general education, self-studies indicated that the writing-to-learn and learning-to-write strategies did not translate into well-developed, higher-order thinking abilities. Like faculty at most undergraduate institutions, we were not eliciting the kinds of higher-order thinking skills defined as our desired program and course outcomes. Our academic culture needed to shift to focus consciously and collectively on our goals and use effective means to encourage students toward the desired levels of achievement.

The Washington State University Critical Thinking Project brings together faculty in a cross-disciplinary collaboration to improve students' higher-order thinking abilities through the improvement of faculty practice. The project helps faculty combine assessment with instruction to increase coherence and promote higher-order thinking, and it encourages improvement of faculty teaching and evaluative practices in a four-year general education curriculum at a large Research-I public university. Ongoing support is provided for faculty to implement innovative combinations of teaching and assessment methods in individual courses—the three tiers of general education courses spanning all disciplines and departments—and on an institution-wide and statewide level.

Fostering critical thinking skills in undergraduates across a university's curriculum presents formidable difficulties. Making valid, reliable, and fine-grained assessments of students' progress in achieving these higher-order intellectual skills involves another set of obstacles. Finally, providing faculty with the tools necessary to refocus their teaching to encourage these abilities in students represents yet another formidable problem. WSU's Critical Thinking Project addresses these three sets of problems simultaneously through one concerted strategy.

In 1996, WSU's Campus Writing Programs, Center for Teaching, Learning and Technology, and the General Education Program collaborated to develop a seven-dimension critical-thinking rubric derived from scholarly work, including Toulmin (1958), Paul (1990), Facione (1990), and local practice and expertise, to provide a process for improving and a means for measuring students' higher-order thinking skills during the course of their college careers (see Exhibit 1; also see http://wsuctproject. wsu.edu/ctr.htm). The intent was to develop a fine-grained diagnostic of student progress as well as to provide a means for faculty to reflect on and revise their own instructional goals, assessments, and teaching strategies. The rubric can be used both as an instructional guide and as an evaluative tool. We use a six-point scale for evaluation, combining ETS scoring methodology with expert-rater methodology (Haswell and Wyche, 1996; Haswell, 1998). The WSU Critical Thinking Rubric identifies seven key areas of critical thinking:

- Identification of a problem or issue
- Establishment of a clear perspective on the issue
- Recognition of alternative perspectives
- Recognition of fundamental assumptions implicit in or stated by the representation of an issue
- Identification and evaluation of evidence
- Location of the issue within an appropriate context(s)
- Assessment of potential conclusions, implications, and consequences

A fully developed process or skill set for thinking critically demonstrates competence with and integration of all these components of formal, critical analysis.

Most of the current work on critical thinking centers on evaluating student performance on standardized tests separate from classroom experience. This approach disconnects evaluation from instruction and is top-heavy with definitions and assessment measures, often promoting a "one way, how to" method for teaching higher-order thinking. This approach yields critical thinking courses, separate from the rest of the undergraduate curriculum, which students take to learn the skill of "how to think." In such programs, the responsibility of teaching higher-order thinking rests in the hands of a single department and engages or affects very few faculty members.

The WSU Critical Thinking Project locates assessment directly within an instructional context and places the responsibility of fostering critical thinking with all faculty and students, making it integral to every classroom experience. Faculty are encouraged to adapt the WSU Critical Thinking Rubric to suit their instructional style, values, and disciplinary expectations. They create assignments and evaluation criteria that promote higher-order thinking abilities within specific contexts. No one person or department on campus is responsible for teaching critical thinking; it is everyone's job. With the Critical Thinking Rubric as a unifying influence, everyone is empowered to define expectations contextually and relevantly. Emphasis is on direct production and evaluation of student learning situated in classroom experience.

**Exhibit 1. Guide to Rating Critical-Thinking Rubric,
Washington State University 2001**

[© 2001, the Center for Teaching, Learning, and Technology, the General Education Program, and the Writing Center, Washington State University.]

1. Identifies and summarizes the **problem or question at issue** (and the source's position).

Scant
   Does not identify and summarize the problem; is confused or identifies a different and inappropriate problem.
   Does not identify or is confused by the issue, or represents the issue inaccurately.

Substantially Developed
   Identifies the main problem and subsidiary, embedded, or implicit aspects of the problem and identifies them clearly, addressing their relationships to each other.
   Identifies not only the basics of the issue, but recognizes nuances of the issue.

2. Identifies and presents the *student's own* **perspective and position** as it is important to the analysis of the issue.

Scant
   Addresses a single source or view of the argument and fails to clarify the established or presented position relative to one's own.
   Fails to establish other critical distinctions.

Substantially Developed
   Identifies, appropriately, one's own position on the issue, drawing support from experience and information not available from assigned sources.

3. Identifies and considers *other* salient **perspectives and positions** that are important to the analysis of the issue.

Scant
   Deals only with a single perspective and fails to discuss other possible perspectives, especially those salient to the issue.

Substantially Developed
   Addresses perspectives noted previously and additional diverse perspectives drawn from outside information.

4. Identifies and assesses the key **assumptions**.

Scant
   Does not surface the assumptions and ethical issues that underlie the issue, or does so superficially.

Substantially Developed
   Identifies and addresses the validity of the key assumptions and ethical dimensions that underlie the issue.

5. Identifies and assesses the **quality of supporting data or evidence** and provides additional data or evidence related to the issue.

Scant
   Merely repeats information provided, taking it as truth, or denies evidence without adequate justification.

Confuses associations and correlations with cause and effect.

Does not distinguish between fact, opinion, and value judgments.

Substantially Developed

Examines the evidence and source of evidence; questions its accuracy, precision, relevance, and completeness.

Observes cause and effect and addresses existing or potential consequences.

Clearly distinguishes between fact and opinion, and acknowledges value judgments.

6. Identifies and considers the influence of the **context*** on the issue.

Scant

Discusses the problem only in egocentric or sociocentric terms.

Does not present the problem as having connections to other contexts—cultural, political, and so on.

Substantially Developed

Analyzes the issue with a clear sense of scope and context, including an **assessment of the audience** of the analysis.

Considers other pertinent contexts.

7. Identifies and assesses **conclusions, implications, and consequences**.

Scant

Fails to identify conclusions, implications, and consequences of the issue or the key relationships between the other elements of the problem, such as context, implications, assumptions, or data and evidence.

Substantially Developed

Identifies and discusses conclusions, implications, and consequences, considering. context, assumptions, data, and evidence.

Objectively reflects on own assertions.

---

*Contexts for Consideration

Cultural/social

Group, national, ethnic behavior or attitudes

Scientific

Conceptual, basic science, scientific method

Educational

Schooling, formal training

Economic

Trade, business concerns, costs

Technological

Applied science, engineering

Ethical

Values

Political

Organizational or governmental

Personal Experience

Personal observation, informal character

We work with faculty to help them create meaningful adaptations of critical thinking practices for their courses. Faculty from all areas of the university— from the sciences as well as the arts, humanities, and social sciences—have found the WSU Critical Thinking Rubric applicable to their definitions of critical thinking and usable in their disciplines. We anticipated that definitions of critical thinking would be discipline-specific or politically charged. To avoid ideological conflicts, we introduced the rubric as a diagnostic guide for faculty to freely adapt to their own pedagogical methods. They are invited to make revisions and alterations relevant to their specific contexts.

The Critical Thinking Project encourages faculty to consider the demographics of students in their courses and to adapt their instructional and evaluative practices based on students' different learning styles. Likewise, the project encourages faculty to articulate their expectations to students overtly. In traditional classroom settings, students often must decipher the instructor's implicit, unstated expectations. Many faculty indicate that they feel as if they are cheating if they give students an articulated set of course expectations. For students from diverse cultures, from outside mainstream academic culture, and especially for at-risk students, this indirectness presents a significant obstacle. Having a clear set of expectations provides these students with a map to navigate the course and a common language for dialogue with the instructor.

The Critical Thinking Project also allows faculty to highlight the types of abilities they wish to promote in their courses, encouraging them to go beyond the information-retrieval assignments that permeate many undergraduate courses. By fostering abilities such as consideration of various perspectives and assumptions underlying an issue or its context, students are encouraged to become engaged with course material on a level that promotes recognition of complexity and variety in the world.

Since 1999, more than 260 WSU faculty from across the disciplines have incorporated the Critical Thinking Rubric into their instructional and evaluative practices. More than 80 faculty from across the disciplines have been trained as evaluators, using the Critical Thinking Rubric. We have collected over 2,400 samples of student work. In addition, we have sponsored three faculty retreats focusing on the promotion of critical thinking through classroom practices. At these gatherings, we have met with more than 200 faculty from 24 institutions in Washington State, and 8 from 4 institutions outside Washington State. We have conducted numerous workshops in national and international forums. In the summer of 2003, we will hold a workshop with K–20 educators in Washington State to explore critical thinking expectations from sandbox to mortarboard and promote more coherence between K–12 and college-level expectations.

Faculty participants have indicated their appreciation for learning "how to explain, recognize, and assess components of critical thinking." They also have come to see that "critical thinking can be approached from multiple perspectives. Assignments don't need to cover all outcomes at one time; they can be varied throughout the course." In one faculty member's view, "using the Critical Thinking Rubric will help me generate assignments as well as guide and assess student work in a meaningful way." Unanimously, participants feel that the Critical Thinking Project has helped clarify their expectations of students and that their use of the rubric in instruction and evaluation has improved their students' critical thinking abilities. Faculty have noted that their participation has helped them "clarify [previously] vague evaluation criteria"; help students learn to "synthesize [their own] comments to highlight key issues"; "ask questions to encourage elaboration and clarification" and "establish a community" based on academic engagement. Furthermore, individual WSU departments, including Management Information Systems and Veterinary Medicine, have made programwide articulations of critical thinking expectations as a result of participation in our project. These departments and programs strive to build critical thinking expectations into all aspects of their curricula.

Integrating the WSU Critical Thinking Rubric and methodology into teaching practices and assignments makes a significant difference in students' higher-order thinking abilities. In a pilot study, we ascertained that students' critical thinking scores increased dramatically in a course that overtly integrated the Critical Thinking Rubric into instructional expectations compared with performances in a course that did not. Papers were rated from two different semesters of the same course (Entomology 401, Biological Thought and Invertebrates) that were taught by the same instructor—one semester when the rubric was not used ($n = 14$) and the following semester when the rubric was used ($n = 12$). The overall mean score (on a 6-point scale; even numbers are used as benchmarks, 2 [weak] to 6 [strong]) in the semester without the rubric, 1.867 (SD = .458), increased significantly to 3.48 (SD = .923, $p = .001$) in the semester when the rubric was used.

Similar gains were reported in other studies involving courses that implemented the rubric as opposed to those that did not. In one study, 123 student essays were assessed from several lower- and upper-division undergraduate courses. In the four courses where the rubric was used variously for instruction and evaluation ($n = 87$), the papers received significantly higher critical thinking ratings than the papers in the four courses in which the rubric was not used ($n = 36$). The mean score for courses in which the rubric was not used was 2.44 (SD = .595), compared to 3.3 (SD = .599, $p = .001$) in courses that employed the rubric. Furthermore, students' critical thinking scores improved more in one semester in courses that used the rubric (average difference of 1.24) than in the regular progression of courses between freshman and junior years (an average difference of .46), as established by comparing entry and junior-level performances in WSU's Writing Assessment Program.

By appreciating and building on the expertise of our faculty, we are able to develop innovative combinations of assessment and instruction, and allow these practices to play out where it matters most—in the classroom. By having faculty align their expectations with their practices, we help faculty retain control over the types of assessment measures they use, and we continue to strive to improve our institution's practice as well. And by developing and employing a measure that evaluates actual student learning outcomes—that is, work products from classes—we are able to provide accountability data without disrupting the university's efforts to provide a world-class education.

For more information on this project, visit our Web site at <http:// wsuctproject.wsu.edu>.

References

Facione, P. A. *Critical Thinking: A Statement of Expert Consensus for Purposes of Educational Assessment and Instruction. Research Findings and Recommendations.* 1990. ERIC Document Reproduction Service: ED 315423.

Haswell, R. H., "Multiple Inquiry in the Validation of Writing Tests." *Assessing Writing,* 1998, 5(1), 89–108.

Haswell, R. H., and Wyche, S. "A Two-Tiered Rating Procedure for Placement Essays." In T. W. Banta, J. P. Lund, K. E. Black, and F. W. Oblander (eds.), *Assessment in Practice: Putting Principles to Work on College Campuses.* San Francisco: Jossey-Bass, 1996.

Paul, R. *Critical Thinking: How to Prepare Students for a Rapidly Changing World.* Santa Rosa, CA: Foundation for Critical Thinking, 1990.

Toulmin, S. E. *The Uses of Argument.* New York: Cambridge University Press, 1958.

In 2003, Diane Kelly-Riley was director of the writing assessment program at Washington State University, Pullman, Washington.

Assessing Students' Moral Awareness

James JF Forest, Bruce Keith

Look for: Multiple measures, both direct and indirect, of cadets' moral awareness developed and administered by faculty at the United States Military Academy at West Point. From Assessment Update 16:1 (2004).

The United States Military Academy (USMA) provides cadets with a liberal education designed to develop versatile and critical thinkers who can adapt to the professional and ethical challenges they will confront. Cadets' moral development is integrated throughout their West Point experience, to the point of being included as one of the USMA's academic program goals.

The Learning Model

Moral awareness requires one to be cognitively attentive to the presence of moral issues and adept at developing options in response to these issues. The framework for developing a cadet's moral awareness is derived from four statements that describe our expectations for their abilities at graduation. In particular, USMA graduates should be able to demonstrate understanding and proficiency in the identification and examination of moral implications related to various situations; rationally analyze specific ethical responses to moral problems; recognize moral issues that arise in their units and help others to gain an understanding of these issues; and work to strengthen the moral respectability of the Army.

Drawn from this framework is a learning model that reflects a curricular structure, a developmental process, and relevant content, which we have integrated throughout the core curriculum to ensure that cadets are engaged in moral discourse. Within the ubiquitous domain of moral awareness at West Point, the academic program outlines a three-part structure that incorporates (1) *recognition*—learning to identify, describe, and analyze moral issues; (2) *moral considerations*—grappling with ethical options, counterarguments, validity, soundness, reasonableness, and implications of competing views; and (3) *application in decision making*—demonstrating cogency, coherence, and consistency of ethical considerations in the moral issue under discussion.

The learning model also articulates a process that describes how cadets proceed through this structure—that is, the various developmental challenges we place before them. Cadets' initial discussions about issues of moral significance center on recognition of the issue, the various moral considerations, and the ways in which ethical responses affect decision making. These discussions incorporate moral motivation, emphasizing why cadets ought to act ethically. As they advance in their understanding of moral and ethical issues, cadets confront the argumentative nature of moral discourse, seeking out the facts of the case, the moral considerations that apply to the facts, and the morally acceptable responses that offer the greatest merit. The developmental structure of the learning model ensures that cadets encounter these questions sequentially through coursework in the core curriculum and the major programs.

Within the context of these learning experiences, the academic curriculum at West Point places considerable emphasis on moral and ethical development. Courses in philosophy, general psychology, and military leadership develop cadets' understanding of the language, arguments, and methods of moral discourse. Additional core courses provide cadets with opportunities to recognize and respond to moral imperatives within political, legal, and economic dimensions of behavior. These courses, combined with their leadership experiences in military applications, encourage cadets to engage in critical thinking, the study of ethical theories, and analysis of moral issues, especially those involving war and the role of society in war. These learning experiences also focus on the leader's influence on individuals and examine the uses of law, the limits of law, the role of law in society, and the distinction between legality and morality. Through this combination of structure, process, and content, the USMA's faculty have designed and implemented a learning model that seeks to ensure a high level of moral and ethical situational awareness among our graduates.

Outcomes Assessment

The Moral Awareness Goal Team, a multidisciplinary group of faculty, maintains principal ownership of the design and assessment of this goal. Their work is supported and reviewed by faculty through the Assessment Steering Committee and the dean. To assess cadets' achievement of the moral awareness goal, this goal team has developed a rubric to represent the standard of performance we expect cadets to achieve. Our assessment initiatives seek to determine the extent to which graduates have reached this standard—namely, their ability to reflect on the moral implications of situations they encounter on and off duty; to examine the consequences of various responses to moral problems in terms of logical consistency and conduciveness to the success of a mission; to work with others to find reasoned, ethical solutions to problems; and, recognizing their own fallibility, to refine their moral sensibility continually and to share their insights with fellow soldiers openly.

Our assessment of the moral awareness goal involves a triangulation of data, including an analysis of survey responses, student course products, and employer feedback. Our review of longitudinal survey data reveals that cadets' confidence in their achievement of the moral awareness goal increases significantly during their four-year experience at West Point, particularly when they are asked to describe their ability to "recognize moral issues in a military situation" and "select morally justifiable actions." Additional assessment evidence, to be provided by content analyses of written essays, research papers, formal presentations, and other course products, will offer other perspectives on cadets' achievement of this goal.

Surveys administered to USMA graduates and their employers (typically unit field commanders) consistently reveal that both the graduates and their commanders are confident in our graduates' abilities to recognize ethical issues and demonstrate morally appropriate decision-making strategies. Furthermore, cadets, graduates, and their commanders consistently report a level of achievement for the moral awareness goal that surpasses that associated with any other goal in the academic program. In addition, the assessment evidence we gather through focus group interviews of former battalion commanders suggests that USMA graduates routinely consider the moral imperatives of their own actions and of those within their units.

The Military Academy has spent the past several years working through an iterative process to assess cadets' achievement of the moral awareness goal. Our analysis of the assessment data gathered through these activities indicates that USMA graduates perform very well on the moral and ethical dimension of the overarching academic program goal of enabling graduates to anticipate and respond effectively to the uncertainties of a changing technological, social, political, and economic world. Furthermore, we are convinced that these efforts are yielding positive results, in terms of improving our curriculum and moving USMA toward an academic culture of long-term assessment renewal. Nonetheless, we have not reached and perhaps will not reach an end state; we are learning valuable lessons as we move forward with this initiative. Annual analyses of the data we have gathered have led us to revise questionnaire items and the overall assessment process. Perhaps one of the most important lessons learned thus far is that assessment is a process—a continual cycle of gathering information, assessing it, examining the methodological issues, refining the instruments, and then gathering more information. In addition, we have learned the importance of annually gathering evidence from multiple sources, including cadets' coursework and opinions as well as the views of graduates and employers.

Conclusion

West Point affords cadets the intellectual and ethical development necessary to succeed as military officers. Effective leadership of troops across a broad spectrum of Army operations requires a thorough understanding of moral and ethical issues. The assessment data we have gathered to date suggests that USMA cadets and graduates generally achieve the standard we have set for the moral awareness goal. We find that the attention we are giving to a comprehensive assessment process, directed by multidisciplinary goals and teams of faculty, is resulting in positive qualitative change in our academic program and curriculum.

In 2004, James JF Forest was assistant professor and assistant dean for academic assessment, and Bruce Keith was professor and associate dean for academic affairs at the United States Military Academy, West Point, New York.

An Innovative Measurement of Communication Outcomes: Self-Perception

Anne Hummer

Look for: Details on development of an instrument to assess students' perceptions of the development of their communication skills, including the dimensions of (1) self-development, (2) peer and faculty input, and (3) program practice opportunities. Technical qualities of the instrument are treated, as well as program improvements undertaken on the basis of assessment findings. From Assessment Update 10:1 (1998).

Some form of communication is involved in every human interaction. Good communication skills are essential for effective personal and professional development. Thus it is appropriate that communication skills are considered relevant outcome measures by most programs and colleges.

Communication is a multifaceted construct. Typically, verbal and written components are the primary focus of outcome measures, but nonverbal, technical, group dynamics, and listening aspects must also be measured to reflect the complex nature of communication. Mastery of communication skills is essential for successful expression of cognitive skills such as critical thinking.

Portfolios and performance assessment through videotaping are the two most common methods used to assess communication outcomes. Generally these methods focus on either the written or verbal aspects of communication and neglect the other dimensions of this complex skill. The high cost of faculty time to evaluate these strategies is a common drawback and, in the case of performance assessment, the need to develop a simulation that clearly defines the behavior to be measured and the specific criteria to be achieved must be considered.

The lack of a methodology to measure the entire scope of communication, and problems with portfolios and performance assessment have led faculty to consider other options. An extensive review of literature failed to provide substantive alternatives. Pace's College Student Experience Questionnaire (1990) provides data related to quality of effort and the achievement of educational goals and supports a connection between the validity of student self-report of cognitive gains and actual knowledge gains. Astin's report (1993) on twenty years of experience with the freshman Cooperative Institutional Research Program questionnaire and subsequent follow-up surveys showed that patterns of self-reported outcomes varied consistently by education major, just as directly assessed cognitive outcomes varied. Dollar (1992) reported similar patterns by alumni on national surveys. Baird (1976) conducted an extensive review of primarily course-based studies that compared self-report knowledge gains with actual outcomes. His results suggest that the two do indeed vary together dependably. Therefore, the idea of using self-reports of cognitive gains, specifically communications skill gains, seemed to have potential.

The Instrument

The Student (Graduate) Perception of Communication Skills instrument builds on the concept that self-reports of cognitive skills correlate with actual knowledge gains. The instrument is composed of fifty statements that reflect the whole communication spectrum, self-development components, peer and faculty input on skills, and program practice opportunities. The wording format requires the student or graduate to read the statement carefully, reflect on the behavior, and accurately assess his or her actual achievement level. Achievement on each behavior is rated using a five-point Likert scale from strongly agree to strongly disagree. The mean score and standard deviation for each of the fifty statements are calculated from the ratings of the sample population. Twenty-five of the statements are worded positively and twenty-five negatively. A mean rating of three or above on a positive statement equates with a rating of unsure to disagree; on a negative statement, unsure to agree. The instrument was piloted after several university departments reviewed the instrument to establish content validity. Reliability of the instrument as measured by Cronbach's correlation coefficient has consistently been .90 or above across all population samples.

Tables 1 and 2 identify the ten student or graduate perceived communication strengths and areas needing improvement for the baccalaureate program's sample population (N = 404). The instrument has been used by associate, baccalaureate, and graduate programs at several different college and university sites. The graduate version of the instrument includes several variations that focus on the ability to present research. *Specific* differences among the colleges have been found on computer, speech, and writing requirements (or the lack thereof). The behavior "computer skills are sufficiently effective to prepare class assignments and papers" consistently had the greatest variability in the standard deviation across all populations. Additional research on the instrument using factor analysis revealed that forty-two of the fifty statements load on the first subscale, "communication skills."

Program Improvements

The following are some examples of changes in programs that have occurred as a result of identifying students' perceived needs for improvement:

Table 1. Student-Perceived Communication Strengths

1. Speaking one-to-one creates stress for me.

2. I adjust my communication techniques to fit the listener(s).

3. I am able to effectively participate in group discussions.

4. I utilize suggestions from faculty feedback on papers to improve my writing skills.

5. I utilize feedback from faculty to improve my oral communication skills.

6. My oral communication skills enable me to feel confident.

7. I adjust my written communications to meet the needs of the reader(s).

8. I utilize suggestions from peer evaluations to improve my communication skills.

9. My writing skills positively influence my academic achievement.

10. I am able to correctly use APA format.

Table 2. Student-Perceived Communication Areas That Could Be Improved

1. I experience greater difficulty expressing my ideas in front of a group than in one-to-one situations.

2. A speaker's delivery and/or mannerisms frequently distract me from receiving the message.

3. I frequently read or memorize my presentation.

4. I need more practice in using group process.

5. The program could have offered more opportunities to practice nonverbal communication techniques.

6. I attempt to process every word a speaker says.

7. The program could have offered more opportunities to improve my oral communication skills.

8. Sometimes my presentation style is dull and unpolished.

9. I frequently speak before I think through an idea.

10. I rarely assess the impact of individual group member's behavior in group process.

Frequent one-minute prepared and extemporaneous class presentations are included in courses beginning in the freshman year, with the length of time for the presentation expanded as the students progress through the program, culminating with a thirty-minute presentation in the capstone course. Student presentations are graded on style, nonverbal techniques, logical progression and clarity of ideas, and delivery, with emphasis on continuous improvement. Part of the grading of presentations is derived from peer evaluations. This technique helps students recognize different style and delivery patterns and become more accustomed to and accepting of diverse patterns. In addition, students indicate that peer input facilitates personal improvement. Grading criteria state that points will be deducted if the presentation is read. Guest speakers and video clips expose students to different lecturers and enhance acceptance of diversity in presentation style. Faculty consistently ask students to summarize a concept just presented, thereby enhancing student synthesis of the concept rather than permitting the perception of a group of disjointed words. Class debates promote clear expression of ideas and the use of group process. Frequent group presentations are required, limited to five to ten minutes, with the requirement that all members participate equally in the presentation. Peer evaluations of each member's presentation and his or her positive and negative contributions to the group are part of the process. Finally, group discussions or debates are conducted that deal with issues related to "difficult colleagues."

Conclusions

In the analysis of student subsamples and total populations, writing skills appear only as a perceived strength; they are not identified as an area needing improvement. Verbal communication and group process skills are consistently identified as areas needing improvement. These student perceptions suggest a need for significant changes in teaching and learning strategies. The importance of feedback from faculty and use of resulting suggestions have emerged as relevant issues. Other behaviors on the instrument have not been identified in this article but are significant to individual colleges and programs. The instrument may be modified to include these local concerns and to address the entire communication process from the perspective of the student learner. Communication reflects the depth of developmental and lifetime opportunities. Although all students are given the same opportunities in each program to develop and refine their communication skills, different outcomes may occur. These outcomes can be influenced by cultural diversity, ethnicity, age, work experience, and previous educational experiences. An extension of this research with a small sample has indicated that significant differences in the perception of communication skills are related to age, gender, and race. The instrument is simple and effective, and it provides colleges and programs with another option for identifying outcomes that facilitate changes that enable all student populations to meet the challenges of interacting in a complex society.

References

Astin, A. W. *What Matters in College?* San Francisco: Jossey-Bass, 1993.

Baird, L. L. "Structuring the Environment to Improve Outcomes." In O. T. Lenning (ed.), *Improving Educational Outcomes.* New Directions for Higher Education, no. 16. San Francisco: Jossey-Bass, 1976.

Dollar, R. "College Influence on Analytical Thinking and Communication Skills of Part-Time Versus Full-Time Students." *College Student Journal*, May/June 1992, pp. 273–279.

Pace, C. R. *The Undergraduates: A Report of Their Activities and Progress in College in the 1980s.* Los Angeles: The Center for the Society of Education, University of California, 1990.

In 1998, Anne Hummer was an associate professor in the College of Health Professions and the coordinator of educational assessment at the University of Detroit Mercy.

Community College Strategies: Using a Capstone Course to Assess General Education Outcomes

Scott Hunt

Look for: Methods developed by a community college faculty to assess valuing diversity outcomes in freshman experience and capstone courses. From Assessment Update 12:2 (2000).

Columbus State Community College (CSCC) is a comprehensive community college offering A.A. and A.S. degrees, over 30 career and technical degree programs, and continuing education and workforce development courses. CSCC is located in the urban setting of Columbus, Ohio, and serves approximately 20,000 students.

Like many community colleges, in the early 1990s CSCC developed a comprehensive assessment plan, both for internal evaluation and improvement and to satisfy North Central Association requirements. As a part of this process, a committee of faculty and administrators, chaired by a faculty member, identified a set of general educational outcomes, which were subsequently adopted by the college at large: (1) critical thinking, (2) problem solving, (3) effective communication, (4) interpersonal skills, (5) valuing diversity, and (6) life skills management.

As these outcomes were being articulated and operationally defined, two new courses in the Arts and Sciences division, Freshman Experience and the Capstone Experience, were designed and adopted, in part to facilitate the general education assessment process.

Specifically, the Freshman Experience course was developed with the intention of introducing students to the expectations of college professors and providing students with the tools to plan their academic path to graduation and transfer from CSCC. The Freshman Experience course was also intended to introduce students to the assessment program of CSCC, especially the general education outcomes. Critical thinking skills were to be introduced in this course through a significant reading, a paper, and discussion of issues. Life skills management and college skills management were a part of this curriculum as well. Time management, test-taking strategies, note-taking strategies, and learning styles were addressed. The course was also to address the written and oral communication rubrics that would subsequently be applied in the students' En-glish classes. Finally, the Freshman Experience course would be the course in which the student portfolio would be explained to students and the portfolio process initiated.

The Capstone Experience course was originally designed to showcase students' development as a result of their experiences at CSCC. The student portfolio is completed in this course, and additional methodologies have been developed to assess the general education outcomes not addressed in the portfolio process.

The remainder of this column will address the design and implementation of a methodology to assess one of those general education outcomes: valuing diversity. Two faculty members from the Social and Behavioral Sciences Department (Karen Muir and Michael Schumacher) accepted responsibility for devising such a process. Since no commercially developed instruments were available, they set out to create an appropriate tool. The evolution of this assessment procedure resulted in a method with many similarities to the procedures developed by Kohlberg and Rest to measure moral development. Kohlberg and Rest assessed college students' level of moral reasoning by asking them to respond to a moral dilemma presented in the form of an anecdote. Subjects indicated their choice of action and their reasons for such action. Subjects' responses were then rated for level of moral development as compared to a previously developed scale.

Similarly, the process developed by Muir and Schumacher simply asks for a student's written statement or response to a dilemma (scenario) that focuses on cultural awareness and understanding. Specifically, the pretest version is given in the Freshman Experience course and the posttest version in the Capstone course. There is a slight difference between the pretest and posttest versions (the scenario changes slightly), but the focus remains on cultural awareness and cultural diversity. Students' responses on both the pretest and posttest versions are holistically scored using a three-point scale (0–2) by two faculty raters. (Inter-rater reliability has been established at .95 and higher.) Preliminary analyses of pilot data using this procedure have yielded promising results, with posttest scores significantly higher than pretest scores. In other words, entry-level students in the Freshman Experience course demonstrated significantly less cultural awareness and understanding than did students at or near graduation. While these results are still tentative, and the pilot project has identified several ways in which both the courses and the assessment process can be improved, college faculty are encouraged by the results. In fact, the General Education Committee has begun a second pilot study to test the efficacy of a similar procedure to assess the interpersonal skills outcome. Affective outcomes such as these, while a part of most community college mission statements and curricula in one form or another, have proven particularly difficult to measure. Thus, the creation of a relatively straightforward methodology for doing so is a welcome addition to our assessment toolbox.

In 2000, Scott Hunt was co-chair of the Faculty Assessment Committee at Columbus State Community College.

Assessment Methods Applicable Across Knowledge and Skills Areas

---

A Multiplicity of Learning: Capstones at Portland State University

Terrel L. Rhodes, Susan Agre-Kippenhan

Look for: The use of reflective essays, end-of-course evaluations, and student focus groups to evaluate a six-credit capstone course in which interdisciplinary student teams apply their learning to respond to a challenge emanating from the community. From Assessment Update 16:1 (2004).

Portland State University (PSU) is a public university with more than twenty-three thousand students enrolled in 120 undergraduate, master's, and doctoral degree programs. Located in downtown Portland, Oregon, PSU is a nationally acclaimed leader in community-based learning. The university's position in the heart of Oregon's economic and cultural center enables PSU students and faculty to apply scholarly theory to the real-world problems of business and community organizations.

In the fall of 1994, the PSU faculty initiated the revised general education program, University Studies. The culmination of this four-year, interdisciplinary general education program is the capstone requirement. Under the guidance of PSU faculty members and community partners, six-credit capstone courses provide community-based learning and give interdisciplinary student teams an opportunity to apply what they have learned in the major and in their other University Studies courses to a challenge emanating from the metropolitan community.

The capstone's purposes are to cultivate in students crucial life abilities that are important both academically and professionally and to allow them to establish connections within the larger community, developing strategies for analyzing and addressing problems and working with others trained in fields different from their own. In the academic year 2002–03, Portland State offered more than 150 capstone courses that engaged some 2,500 students in community work in the Portland area. Each course concludes with the creation of a summative product appropriate to the project. The capstone offerings range from neighborhood revitalization efforts, work with the sheriff's office, graphic design, work with immigrant populations, numerous efforts in schools, performance-based work, and small business initiatives. The capstones represent the involvement of every unit on campus, including two graduate schools and all the professional areas.

Capstone Assessment

Assessment has been an integral part of the capstone courses since their inception in 1997 and even in their earlier pilot stage. Assessment has been both formative and summative and has encompassed a number of different approaches. An end-of-course evaluation has been employed consistently, as have other self-report measures. The data from these efforts have informed practice and have been valuable in program improvement. In 2000, assessment of student work samples provided a more fully realized picture of the courses. This effort led to the development of a common assignment, a brief reflective essay that each student writes to tie course experiences to a program goal. Comprehensive rubrics are used to review the essays, and again, the data collected have contributed to both course and program improvement.

Assessment of capstone courses is particularly challenging because it is important to contextualize student learning and present the complex multidimensional projects in an accessible format. Assessment is concerned not just with end results but also with the process of learning. Second, our assessment work grows from findings that measuring the impact of service learning on students requires collecting data from multiple sources. Major aspects of our multidimensional capstone assessment are summarized below.

Student Focus Group

In 1999–2000, students were asked about their experiences in working with their community partners. It became apparent that some classes had better working relationships with the community partner than others. In the classes where there were not good working relationships, students felt that the communication between the university, the faculty member, and the partner needed to be improved. Students said that good communication was a necessary component of a successful capstone experience. In general, students felt somewhat prepared for their experience in the community. Some students felt uncomfortable at the beginning, but as soon as the expectations of them became clear, they felt less so. The majority of students said that the most important learning experience of their class was completing the community project. Students perceived that their contribution to the community was a direct application of what they had learned in their assigned coursework. They felt that their contribution benefited the community, and this was a major highlight for them.

University Studies Goals and a Common Assignment

In 2001–02, a common assignment was implemented. Students are asked to relate their learning in their capstone course to the University Studies goals. The assessment team agreed on the following prompt: "Please write a three-to-five page analysis summarizing the ways you have gained experience with one of the University Studies goals: communication, critical thinking, variety of human experiences, and social/ethical responsibility. Please focus on one goal, using specific examples from your personal and team experiences with your community partners, within-class discussions and course readings, or in completing your project."

Because most students wrote about two University Studies goals—communication and the variety (diversity) of human experience—these two goals formed the basis of the rubrics created to assess the goals. Early in the spring 2002 term, external reviewers agreed that the resulting scores were lower than expected, but that the common student assignment was a valid way to assess student learning outcomes. Faculty agreed that it was necessary to (1) revise the language used in the rubrics; (2) establish a program for achieving inter-rater reliability; (3) make the rubrics known to the students; (4) include assessment of students' writing as a component of the assignment; and (5) use the University Studies writing rubrics to assess the students' writing ability rather than the separate one that had been developed for the capstones. The revised common assignment was used during 2002–03; results are still being assessed.

Student Self-Reports

End-of-course evaluations are collected in each capstone course. Transfer students enter the University Studies program without having the benefit of the more intensive foundational first year or two of the program that introduces students to the philosophy and goals of the general education program. Thus, student evaluations of capstones include the responses of many transfer students whose exposure to the goals of the program is limited. Nevertheless, the responses of native and transfer students have been quite similar. For example, more than 60 percent of students indicated the following: "I will continue to volunteer or participate in the community after this course"; "the work I performed in the community enhanced my ability to communicate more effectively with multiple audiences"; "the community aspect of the course helped me develop my problem-solving skills"; "the various disciplines and majors of the students in the class helped the team work together in understanding the community issues represented in this capstone"; and "through this course I was made aware of my social and ethical responsibility to myself and to others." More than 70 percent indicated the following: "my participation in this capstone helped me to connect what I learned to real-life situations"; "I feel that the community work I did through this course benefited the community"; "I felt a responsibility to meet the needs of the community partner of this course"; "students in this class had the opportunity to discuss and reflect on our work in the community and were able to connect this with the assigned readings and other course materials"; and "there was a reflective component to this course that enhanced my understanding of my personal strengths and weaknesses."

External Study of Capstones' Impact on Students

In one of the first scholarship of teaching articles on the impact of University Studies in its beginning years, Collier (2000) compared a group of students in the capstone courses with students who had not participated in the University Studies program with regard to their identities as students. He found that University Studies had indeed influenced the role identification and self-concept of students as students. He found that the capstone experience served as a socialization agent and that role identification occurred on all four goal dimensions of the program, to varying degrees. This study suggests that students in the program experience growth in the goal areas, as well as a more fundamental role definition change as leaders in the broader community that may persist after the students have graduated.

For the past four years, a professor in the Graduate School of Education has been conducting a post-capstone student survey (Cress and Brubaker, 2003). Regarding capstone experiences in social and ethical responsibility, the researcher found that eight of ten students said they believed the following: individuals can do something to bring about changes in society; colleges have a responsibility to prepare graduates to become engaged community members; and community-based learning courses help prepare students for the real world. Finally, two-thirds of students (67 percent) believed that colleges should require students to volunteer in order to graduate.

Overall, the data indicated that students make significant educational gains from the beginning to the end of the capstone experience as a result of their community-based learning experiences in capstone courses. Specifically, as a result of participating in capstone courses, students reported gains in the following areas:

- Interpersonal skills
- Leadership ability
- Public speaking ability
- Tolerance of others with different beliefs
- Knowledge of people from different races or cultures
- Understanding of social issues
- Knowledge of how to make a difference in the community
- Desire to volunteer in the future

When the responses were examined in relation to major demographic categories, some interesting findings emerged, with implications for faculty and program providers. For example, older students may be less likely to support the educational concept of community-based learning. Male students may be less likely to want to discuss and negotiate controversial issues. Students of color may have a difficult time seeing how they personally can create change. Data over the four years were impressively consistent.

Conclusion

Assessing capstone courses has been exciting but challenging. We are constantly gathering information both about the courses and about the assessment process. Reflecting on the process has yielded some valuable lessons. We have encountered notable pitfalls, come up with some successful strategies, and have lessons that we can share with others.

In regard to pitfalls and challenges, we note that with a program as varied as the capstone program at Portland State University, it is difficult to create one set of common expectations; however, having common expectations greatly simplifies assessment. Likewise, it is difficult to use just one assessment approach. As with all assessment, it must be meaningful to faculty and students, and in this case, program assessment must be aligned with other course goals.

Our successful strategies are in some ways corollaries of our pitfalls. Capstone assessment is most successful when program assessment and course goals align. We need variety and flexibility in our approaches to address the needs of the specific capstone project experiences. And while we want to accommodate the individual needs of the course, we need consistency of language about goals for student learning and course objectives in order to draw conclusions across the program and develop assessment tools that can be applied to multiple courses.

We have some lessons that we can share as well. Capstone assessment is messy, with many fits and starts, and lengthy, with each successive plan drawing on the one before it. It is clear that multiple approaches, both qualitative and quantitative, are needed. A workable assessment process needs faculty participation at all stages and in all aspects of development, implementation, and analysis. We need to pay close attention to student context and consistent student-centered language. And while the assessment process is valuable in measuring personal development, there is a need for multiple pedagogies and strategies to address the specific needs of student populations differentiated on the basis of race, ethnicity, gender, and age.

Our lessons, strategies, and pitfalls have a common finding. We have seen the value of the program assessment approach in helping us gather aggregate data to enhance student learning as well as in extending the value of the individual courses, projects, and student experiences.

References

Collier, P. J. "The Effects of Completing a Capstone Course on Student Identity." *Sociology of Education*, Oct. 2000, 73, 285–299.

Cress, C. M., with Brubaker, T. "2002–2003 Capstone Student Assessment." Unpublished manuscript, Aug. 2003.

In 2004, Terrel L. Rhodes was vice provost for curriculum and undergraduate studies, and Susan Agre-Kippenhan was chair and professor of art at Portland State University.

Closing the Feedback Loop in Classroom-Based Assessment

Barbara E. Walvoord, Barbara Bardes, Janice Denton

Look for: Examples of using classroom assessment to improve not only individual classes and courses but also departments, divisions, and institutions. Using Primary Trait Analysis in developing scoring rubrics is discussed. From Assessment Update 10:5 (1998).

The classroom teaching, learning, testing, and grading process, when well conducted by faculty, can yield rich information about student learning. When faculty members set clear classroom-learning objectives, construct exams and assignments that teach and test that learning, help students to learn what is needed, use clear criteria and standards to assess student performance, and then make pedagogical changes based on those data, they are meeting many of the guidelines for good assessment set by regional accreditors and national organizations. As isolated artifacts—when no one knows what they mean—grades are not useful for departmental or institutional assessment. But the power of teachers to generate information about learning in the classroom and to institute changes based on that information make classroom assessment highly attractive to institutions of higher education.

To serve institutional assessment needs, classroom assessment must be high quality, criteria and standards must be explicit, assessment measures and outcomes must be made public in ways not commonly used in the past, and the feedback loop must be closed (Walvoord and Anderson, 1998). In this article we explore the last condition. Regional accreditors require that in an assessment plan the institution must close the feedback loop—that is, *it must use assessment information to make changes* that are intended to enhance student learning. Not closing the loop is one of the most frequent criticisms of institutional assessment plans identified by the North Central Association's accrediting teams (Lopez, 1996). Further, for its own self-improvement and to make its assessment efforts worthwhile, the college or university wants to know how it can use classroom-generated data at the department and institutional levels to improve learning.

Closing the Feedback Loop at the Classroom Level

There are actually three feedback loops that must be closed: the class-room, the department, and the institution. It is important to identify the information and the actions appropriate to each loop.

We illustrate the three loops with an actual case: the assessment of critical thinking in general education at Raymond Walters College (RWC), a two-year open-admissions branch campus of the University of Cincinnati. RWC is so autonomous that it is accredited independently, in a different year, from the main campus. Located in a Cincinnati sub-urb, RWC has 105 full-time faculty, 130 adjuncts, and 2,100 full-time-equivalent students. Except for a writing course, there are no separately identifiable collegewide general education courses; rather, general edu-cation goals are to be met by elements embedded within the curriculum offered by each program or department. RWC students have widely vary-ing goals. They drop in and out, transfer, take classes on other campuses, or take only a few courses. Thus the beginning and ending points of a stu-dent's program at RWC are difficult to pinpoint for assessment. As in many institutions of higher education, individual departments and pro-grams exercise considerable curricular and pedagogical autonomy.

In this setting, the college's Academic Assessment Committee (AAC)—a faculty committee charged with implementing assessment and reporting to the accrediting association—decided to assess the general education goal of critical thinking. Given the conditions we have de-scribed, however, it was nearly impossible to assess whether some type of generic critical thinking, common to all disciplines, improved in all students between some presumed beginning point and some presumed ending point. Further, after piloting a standardized test of critical think-ing, RWC faculty pointed out that the generic test did not reflect well the discipline-specific critical thinking they taught in their classrooms. Thus there was no way to get faculty to try to teach students to do better on the test. In other words, RWC faculty rejected standardized tests in part because it would have been difficult or impossible to close the feedback loop at the classroom level—that is, to use test results to improve classroom learning.

The AAC therefore decided to base its approach on the recognition that critical thinking is discipline-specific: it appears to be somewhat different in a philosophy class than in a chemistry or nursing class, and it operates in conjunction with discipline-specific knowledge (Perkins, 1987). Even within a single discipline, modes of critical thinking may vary (Herrington, 1983). Thus the AAC allowed the definition of critical thinking to emerge from classroom practice and from classroom assessment conducted by faculty, who were the college's experts on critical thinking in their respective disciplines. The feedback loop would first be closed at the classroom level. Then the departmental and institutional levels would receive information and take action appropriate to their powers and roles.

Accordingly, the AAC recommended, and the faculty voted, that each full-time faculty member would submit the following for departmental and institutional discussion: (1) one of his or her classroom assignments or exams that tested critical thinking in his or her discipline; (2) a detailed scoring rubric, in the form of a Primary Trait Analysis (PTA), explained in Walvoord and Anderson (1998); (3) aggregated student scores using the rubric; and (4) an indication of how the faculty member intended to use the students' scores to make changes in the classroom that would help students improve their critical thinking skills. The committee did not dictate the content of the scoring rubric, only the format. Thus a scoring rubric could include "support for claims" in philosophy or "controlling variables" in biology. By fall 1996, 90 percent of the full-time faculty had submitted these materials. (In later stages, RWC will bring adjunct faculty into this process.) Because faculty constructed the assignments and tests, composed the rubrics using their own standards and criteria, and assessed students' critical thinking skills using the faculty members' own rubrics, there was strong incentive to use the data (the students' scores) as a diagnostic tool to lead to changes in teaching strategies. In workshops and poster sessions that the college sponsored, in presentations to their colleagues, and in interviews, faculty attested to the power of classroom-based assessment to help them improve their teaching. Though it is too soon to tell whether the performance of RWC students is improving over time, Anderson and Walvoord (1991) have documented significant improvement in student performance when teachers assess student learning using PTA, use that information diagnostically, and change their teaching methods. Faculty involvement in closing the loop at the classroom level is one of the most important strengths of RWC's classroom-based model.

Closing the Loop at the Department and Institutional Levels

But how shall the feedback loop be closed at the levels above the classroom? This problem is different in a classroom-based approach such as that of RWC than in more centralized approaches to general education assessment. When an institution administers a standardized test, or when a central body or committee examines students' portfolios of work from a variety of courses, administrators and the central committee know the data first and most completely, and then must get the classroom teachers to be informed and to buy into the assessment initiative. In the RWC scheme, the classroom teachers know the data earliest and most thoroughly, and because they own it they have strong incentives to act on it. The strategy for closing the loop at higher levels is to consider what information these higher levels need and what actions are appropriate for providing that information. In such a decentralized system, the roles of the department and the institution are (1) to ensure that good assessment is taking place at the lower levels, (2) to support the initiatives for change that arise from the lower levels, and (3) to identify and address problems that require departmental or institutional solutions. To fulfill these functions, departments and central administrators do not need to know or dictate every single classroom change. Only certain kinds of information need to be passed up the line. For example, if a teacher examines her students' performance using the PTA scores and changes her pedagogy accordingly, the department and institution need to know that such assessment is taking place, but they do not need to know actual scores or to tell the teacher what to do. Departmental and central administrators support the teacher if resources or advice are needed, and they address common and systemic problems that can be handled best at the departmental or institutional level.

Following this approach, the RWC's AAC asked each department to hold one end-of-year department meeting in which faculty members presented and discussed their classroom assignments, rubrics, and aggregated student scores; their analyses of the data; and any changes they planned for enhancing students' critical thinking skills. The department then reported to the AAC what had happened at the meeting, using a set of questions suggested by the AAC.

Not every classroom action by individual teachers needed department-level action. Sometimes faculty simply reported that they had identified a problem and changed their teaching in certain ways. But some issues identified in the classroom assessment required department-level action. The departmental conversations were intended (1) to ensure that teachers felt peer pressure to conduct assessment and to document that they had done so, (2) to address problems that were common to a number of teachers or rooted in departmental structures, and (3) to report to the AAC.

The final level for closing the loop was the central administrative level. The two parties most involved were the AAC and the dean. The AAC collected the departmental reports of the meetings at which the classroom assessments were discussed. The AAC used these materials to identify common problems that could then be communicated to the dean and the faculty with appropriate recommendations for action, and to write an institution-wide report for the North Central Association. The report could not say that RWC students had risen or fallen on some centralized measure of generic critical thinking. Rather, the report documented that instructors were measuring students' critical thinking skills, analyzing the results, and closing the feedback loop in their classrooms and departments, and that the institution was receiving information and taking action appropriate to its role in a highly decentralized system.

The dean, who is the chief executive officer, is ex officio on the AAC, has access to the committee's files on request, and of course sees the files as they are made available to outside accreditors. But the dean did not review the individual faculty members' reports or review the departmental reports before the assessment committee prepared its summary. This deliberate hands-off policy helped to reassure faculty that the assessment process was completely outside the loop of individual personnel decisions. The dean did have an important role, however, in supporting initiatives and changes that arose from individuals and departments. Some individuals came for help on a specific project that had been spurred by their classroom assessment. Departments came, too. For example, one departmental delegation came to tell the dean, "We have good news and bad news. The good news is, we love this process of developing scoring rubrics and using them. The bad news is, the process has showed us that we need to develop a new curriculum, and we need resources to do it." The dean also acts on recommendations from the AAC to identify institution-level problems arising from the individual and departmental reports.

In sum, then, the RWC process focuses on closing the feedback loop at three levels: the classroom, the department, and the institution (including the dean and the AAC). Because the classroom teachers are the ones who shape and collect the data (under guidelines issued by the AAC), they know the data earliest and most thoroughly, and they are strongly motivated to act on it. This powerful process, employed by 90 percent of the full-time faculty, is a great strength of the RWC classroom-based approach. It ensures that several of the requirements for good assessment—faculty buy-in, assessment of relevant skills that are actually being taught, student participation and motivation, and assessment over time in a learning context—will be met. The department's and institution's roles are not to know the data earliest and best but rather to ensure that teachers know it, to ensure that classroom assessment procedures are strong, to support initiatives for change arising from teachers, to identify and act on problems that demand departmental or institution-wide solutions, and to document these activities for accreditors and other external audiences.

References

Anderson, V. J., and Walvoord, B. E. *Thinking and Writing in College: A Study of Students in Four Disciplines.* Urbana, IL: National Council of Teachers of English, 1991.

Herrington, A. *Writing in an Academic Setting: A Study of the Rhetorical Contexts for Writing in Two College Chemical Engineering Courses.* Doctoral dissertation, Language, Literature, and Communication Department, Rensselaer Polytechnic Institute, 1983. (University Microfilms no. 840–9508).

Lopez, C. L. *Opportunities for Improvement: Advice from Consultant-Evaluators on Programs to Assess Student Learning.* Chicago, IL: North Central Association of Colleges and Schools, Commission on Institutions of Higher Education, 1996.

Perkins, D. N. "Thinking Frames: An Integrative Perspective on Teaching Cognitive Skills." In J. B. Baron and R. J. Sternberg (eds.), *Teaching Thinking Skills: Theory and Practice.* New York: Freeman, 1987.

Walvoord, B. E., and Anderson, V. G. *Effective Grading: A Tool for Learning and Assessment.* San Francisco: Jossey-Bass, 1998.

In 1998, Barbara E. Walvoord was director of the John Kaneb Center for Teaching and Learning at the University of Notre Dame, Barbara Bardes was dean of Raymond Walters College of the University of Cincinnati, and Janice Denton was associate professor of chemistry and chair of the Academic Assessment Committee at Raymond Walters College of the University of Cincinnati.

Community College Strategies: The Butler County Community College Individualized Student Assessment Pilot Project

Phil Speary

Look for: Basing assessment of general education for community college students on classroom-based measures of their personal development, analytical thinking, communication, and technological (PACT) skills. Standardized instruments and scoring rubrics enable assessment office staff to aggregate students' scores across courses for each of the PACT skills. From Assessment Update 14:3 (2002).

Contemporary advances in the assessment of students' achievement of learning outcomes are prompting a reevaluation of the merit of traditional methods of documenting individual student performance. The process of letter grades assigned at the end of a course averaged together to compute a grade point average and printed in chronological sequence to produce a traditional transcript yields no clear information about what exactly a student has achieved in terms of learning outcomes. Letters and aggregate numbers seem to be of more significance than what learning has actually taken place. Potential employers find transcripts of little use because they bear no clear, specific evidence of students' development of desired abilities and skills.

The Learning Outcomes Project

A Community College Strategies column in the November–December 2001 issue of *Assessment Update* documented Butler County Community College's ongoing process of assessing general education outcomes across the curriculum on an aggregate basis. In addition to that effort, Butler

County Community College (BCCC) is also participating in the League for Innovation 21st Century Learning Outcomes Project, which began in fall 2000. The 21st Century Learning Outcomes Project involves assessment and documentation of individual students' achievement of learning outcomes that have been identified as crucial for success in the twenty-first century. Out of this piloting process, it is hoped that practical models for such individualized assessment of students at the community college level will emerge.

The BCCC Learning PACT

In spring 2001, members of the Butler Learning Outcomes Project (LOP) Team revised the complex list of learning outcomes it had been employing for several years to form a new compact format called the Butler Learning PACT. PACT is an acronym that represents the major categories of learning outcomes included in the Butler model:

P = *Personal Development Skills*
  • Self-concept
  • Health management
  • Time management
  • Coping with change
  • Effective relationships
  • Teamwork
  • Valuing diversity
  • Effective citizenship
  • Ethical conduct
  • Leadership

A = *Analytical Thinking Skills*
  • Problem solving
  • Critical thinking
  • Historical interpretation
  • Aesthetic response

C = *Communication Skills*
- Reading
- Writing
- Listening
- Speaking
- Nonverbal communication

T = *Technological Skills*
- Computer literacy
- Internet use
- Field-related technology

The Butler LOP Team is overseeing the piloting of individualized assessment of student achievement in all of these skill areas through activities conducted in representative courses from all discipline areas, augmented by observation and interview processes focusing on various student activity programs. This pilot process will continue over the next several years.

Beginning the Pilot Process

Butler began the pilot process in summer semester 2001 with two courses: Basic Principles of Speech (SP 100) and Substance Abuse Awareness (BS 115). Only selected sections of these courses were involved in the summer pilot, in order to keep the size of the project manageable. Faculty teaching those sections selected the specific Learning PACT outcomes to be assessed. They generated the assessment instruments to be used and the standardized rubrics to score student work for those selected outcomes. In fall 2001, the faculty who had conducted the pilot analyzed both the data and the assessment process and then reported to the LOP Team and other faculty in their discipline areas about the pilot. In spring semester 2002, additional sections of SP 100 and BS 115 that were taught by a broader range of full-time and part-time faculty became involved in the ongoing and revised pilot process.

The Speech Pilot

Two faculty members designed the Basic Principles of Speech individualized assessment process. They agreed that various assignments regularly incorporated into the Basic Principles of Speech class could be used as assessment instruments to evaluate students' achievement of learning outcomes for critical thinking, speaking, listening, and teamwork. These faculty also decided to generate new instruments that would assess students' achievement of learning outcomes for health management, time management, and ethical conduct.

The faculty designated the most advanced informative speech assignment and the most advanced persuasive speech assignment as the assessment instruments for critical thinking and speaking. A standardized rubric was then generated for each of those speeches. The criteria used in those rubrics were taken from the course objectives stated in the recently revised Basic Principles of Speech course outline prepared by Butler speech faculty.

When students presented these two speeches, in addition to assigning traditional grades, the instructors scored students' performances using the standardized rubrics. Students' scores for the two speeches were then translated to the Learning PACT critical thinking and speaking rubrics. Thus students' performances on the two speaking assignments could be used as assessment tools indicating their achievement of critical thinking and speaking learning outcomes.

The two pilot faculty members also agreed to use the graded assignments in the course's listening unit as a means of assessing students' achievement of Learning PACT listening learning outcomes. They designated specific speeches to test students' listening comprehension and critical listening skills. Students' responses to the designated speeches were scored using standardized rubrics for listening comprehension and critical listening, which the two faculty had generated on the basis of the Speech 100 course outcomes for listening. Students' scores on these two rubrics were then translated to the Learning PACT rubric for listening.

A standardized teamwork rubric was used to score students' achievement of outcomes for that Learning PACT skill. The two pilot faculty used group tasks assigned in the course's group discussion and problem-solving unit as the assessment instruments for this learning outcome. The faculty observed students as they worked together in groups and used the rubrics to assess students' behavior. One of the faculty also asked students to use the rubrics to conduct self-assessments.

The faculty also wanted to assess students' achievement in three other personal development areas: health management, time management, and ethical conduct. They created a pair of rubrics for each of these areas. The first in each pair is a self-assessment to be completed by the student at the beginning and the end of the semester. The second is to be used by a faculty member at the end of the semester after having observed the student throughout the course. The health management rubrics focus specifically on stress management and performance anxiety.

As the semester progressed, students completed the various assignments that were being used for assessment. All of the assignments were integrated in the normal coursework. No particular emphasis was given to assignments used for assessment; however, the overall process of assessment was presented at the beginning of the semester. The faculty explained the pilot process to the students, emphasizing its potential benefit to them as a record of their achievement of specific learning skills during their participation in the course.

At the end of the semester, the Butler Office of Assessment gathered the assessment instruments, translated the scores for entry under the Learning PACT rubrics, and recorded the results on the student performance records. The Office of Assessment created a document for each participating student that listed their level of achievement in each assessed learning outcome. Students received hard copies of their individual student performance records by mail. Students taking this speech course received not only a letter grade but also a specific record of what they had accomplished in the course in relation to the Butler Learning PACT outcomes.

This pilot individualized assessment of student performance in speech did more than provide documentation of academic achievement for individual students. The Butler Office of Assessment was able to compile aggregate data from all the scores produced from participating students' work. Thus, the assessment office was able to obtain helpful assessment data profiling students' achievement of learning outcomes in critical thinking, speaking, listening, teamwork, health management, time management, and ethical conduct from one complete set of student work. Assessment data were generated through regular assignments integrated in normal coursework rather than from assessment instruments unrelated to students' coursework.

Growth of the Model

The Butler Individualized Student Assessment Pilot has grown significantly since summer 2001. Instructors of courses ranging from Music Theory to Chemistry I to Graphics I and Statistics for the Social Sciences initiated pilot projects similar to the speech pilot in fall semester 2001. In addition, the BCCC choir embarked on a yearlong study of student learning in personal development skills.

Enthusiasm has spread among faculty to the extent that instructors from eighteen discipline areas are either participating in individualized student assessment pilots in spring semester 2002 or are generating action plans for implementation in fall semester 2002. The faculty overseeing the school's newspaper staff are conducting a study of student learning of personal development skills similar to that being conducted with the choir. The Butler coaching staff and director of residence facilities are working with the Office of Assessment to develop similar studies for the football team and the residence hall assistants to begin in fall 2002. The chemistry faculty have expanded their student assessment portfolio pilot to include students' progress through Chemistry II. Lifetime Fitness instructors are implementing student self-assessment and faculty assessment of health management skills. History instructors are piloting assessment of student achievement in critical thinking, historical interpretation, and effective citizenship. The information technology faculty have initiated a pilot project in cooperation with Brainbench, a testing corporation, to create individual e-transcripts that certify students' achievement of a wide range of computer skills. These are just some of the ways in which the Butler pilot project is growing. One of the most encouraging aspects of the project has been the level of faculty interest. As faculty see the direct impact of assessment on students, their enthusiasm for assessment of student learning outcomes dramatically increases.

In 2002, Phil Speary was director of assessment at Butler County Community College, El Dorado, Kansas.

Course-Embedded Assessment: A Teaching Strategy to Improve Student Learning

Donald W. Farmer

Look for: Multiple course-based assessment strategies employed across the disciplines from point of entry to graduation. Faculty discussion of assessment findings in their courses produces institution-wide improvements. From Assessment Update 5:1 (1993).

Faculty at King's College have committed themselves to the concept of assessment as an integral part of the teaching and learning process and as a strategy to improve both the quality and quantity of student learning. Assessment at King's has been designed to promote the development of a new outcomes-oriented core curriculum. Course-embedded assessment strategies are incorporated throughout the curriculum—both in core courses and in major programs. These strategies support and are diagnostic of student learning.

At King's College, students engage in multiple performance-based assessment experiences in the classroom from the point of entry to the point of graduation. Assessment strategies embedded in coursework address directly the issue of student motivation. Students take assessment seriously because it counts as part of their course grades and because they receive meaningful feedback from faculty that both appraises their present performance and coaches them for future success. Faculty also take course-embedded assessment seriously because they are evaluating student learning in the context of their own expectations in the classroom.

Assessment has contributed to student learning at King's by encouraging faculty to make explicit learning goals and criteria for judging student performance and by using strategies to encourage behaviors that contribute to student success. The concept of assessment as learning requires that the criteria for judging student performance be shared with students prior to initiation of the learning process. Assessment criteria serve to clarify for students the qualitative level of faculty expectations. Faculty have always had assessment criteria in mind as they graded essays and exams, but rarely have they shared such criteria publicly with students. During the process of transferring criteria from the recesses of their minds to paper, most faculty discover ambiguities and inconsistencies that they did not know existed. Further reflection on criteria causes faculty to push their thinking beyond the "what" to the "why" of teaching, and beyond content to desired student learning outcomes.

Some King's faculty initially resisted the concept of assessment as learning on the grounds that it would increase workload and interfere with their coverage of course material. But they found that course-embedded assessment strategies do not significantly increase faculty work load because routine assignments and examinations are themselves time-consuming. What does increase is the thinking time required for faculty to design assignments and examination questions capable of assessing more sophisticated learning outcomes. Additional time is also required to write appropriate assessment criteria to guide and to evaluate students in their academic performance. Faculty who assign a high priority to covering material often discover just how little information students retain after they complete a course. Coverage of material frequently occurs at the expense of student understanding of the material. Moreover, projected demands of the information age in the twenty-first century strongly suggest that students need to acquire skills through resource-based learning rather than through prepackaged and predigested material provided in lectures and textbooks. Course-embedded assessment permits faculty to work smarter, not harder.

Components of the Assessment Program

The assessment program at King's has several components. All core curriculum courses use pre- and postassessments, common to all sections of a course, in order to evaluate how students think and communicate in their respective disciplines. The assessments are designed cooperatively by faculty teaching sections of the same course. The postassessment is administered to students two weeks prior to the end of the course in order to provide ample time for faculty to give feedback to students. The postassessment usually counts as 20% of the final examination grade.

Postassessments need not be comprehensive but instead can be focused on a priority goal for the course and designed to reveal the extent to which students can function at a collegiate level within the discipline. For example, in an introductory history course, an essay analyzing conflicting interpretations of a historical event might be assigned to determine if students have moved beyond the mere information level in their study of history.

Competence Growth Plans for eight transferable skills of liberal learning provide another component of the course-embedded assessment model. These skills range from effective writing and speaking to computer and information literacy. The faculty in each major program have designed their plans to include developmental assessment strategies and assessment criteria for evaluating student mastery of transferable skills of liberal learning from freshman through senior levels. Students' performances in these assessment experiences count as part of their grades in a variety of courses. Students experiencing difficulty in meeting the assessment criteria may seek assistance from the Academic Skills Center or from the faculty member teaching the course.

Four-year Competence Growth Plans are developed by faculty in each major program. Since most students cannot master a skill in a single freshman-level course, faculty in each major program must assume responsibility for helping students further develop their skills within the framework of the discipline in their respective major programs. Faculty can accomplish this by designing more challenging assignments and by rethinking the use of class time. For example, the accounting faculty at King's increased from three to four the number of class meetings per week for the sophomore-level intermediate accounting course in order to integrate writing, critical thinking, oral communication, and information literacy strategies with the teaching of accounting. These strategies build on introductory skill courses in general education and help prepare students to meet more sophisticated applications in junior- and senior-level accounting courses.

Another assessment strategy is the Sophomore-Junior Diagnostic Project. Students usually begin their projects in response to an assignment in a second-semester sophomore course in their major field. After receiving feedback from faculty members, students continue to work on their projects during the summer. They submit these projects in a first-semester junior-year course in the major where the projects fulfill requirements of the particular course and are graded. These projects are, however, reviewed by other departmental faculty for assessment purposes.

The Sophomore-Junior Diagnostic Project in political science serves to illustrate how these projects can be discipline-specific while at the same time reflecting appropriate transferable skills of liberal learning. Based on previous coursework in social science methods and American government, majors are asked to design a survey interview instrument for use with individuals in local or regional government that will help to develop a leadership profile of people who become involved in government at that level. Students begin their work in a required sophomore-level course in political science and submit their research project in a required course in the first semester of their junior year. Students can accomplish this project no matter where they reside during the summer. The projects reveal students' command over social science methodology, their knowledge of American local government, and their ability to practice liberal learning skills such as writing, quantitative analysis, oral communication, and information literacy.

The Senior-Level Integrated Assessment takes place within the context of a senior seminar in a student's major field of study. The assessment criteria developed by faculty communicate the expectations of faculty for graduating seniors. These expectations include a common core of concepts and other cognitive content as well as application of skills. The students' grades for the seminar reflect their ability to meet these expectations through a variety of performance-based assessment experiences embedded in the design of each senior seminar.

The marketing department signs an agreement each year with a company seeking to market a new consumer product or to remarket an existing product. The senior marketing majors are divided into rival groups to compete for the marketing contract. Each group of students prepares a complete marketing plan, including all marketing research and financial analysis, and an advertising plan. They present their work in writing to the King's faculty, the head of the company, and the marketing staff. They then make an oral presentation before the same group, supported by multimedia. This project reflects students' command of the content and methodology of the marketing discipline and a variety of transferable liberal learning skills ranging from effective oral and written communication to quantitative analysis and creative thinking. They receive feedback not only from King's faculty but also from the company head and the marketing staff.

Discipline Specific Versus Generic Assessment Design

The King's College model recognizes that faculty in different disciplines have different expectations of students at the point of graduation, as determined by the frameworks of their respective disciplines. Objectives, strategies, and criteria for assessing student learning in each major program are the responsibility of departmental faculty. Faculty who teach courses in major programs build sequentially on the common learning outcomes for students articulated by the faculty teams responsible for courses in the core curriculum. Consequently, linkage is effected between learning in the core curriculum and learning in major fields of study, and such linkage fosters an understanding of the concepts of cumulative and transferable learning.

Although a departmentally based process for assessing desired learning outcomes does not produce uniformity throughout each department, it does result in faculty articulating exit criteria for student majors that make sense to students and to faculty within each discipline. However, the range of desired student learning outcomes among the major programs must be monitored carefully to guarantee that senior-level assessment criteria for Competence Growth Plans and for Senior-Level Integrated Assessments fall within an acceptable range in order to provide a common qualitative definition for a King's College baccalaureate degree. In order to satisfy regional accreditation agency requirements, a sampling technique could be used to select student assessments that reveal work at different performance levels when juxtaposed against faculty assessment criteria. External evaluators are able to engage in a more holistic assessment of student learning by examining actual examples of student performance rather than by relying only on numerical ratings. This leads to consensual validation of learning outcomes.

Classroom Research

Classroom research and assessment that are developed in tandem may be viewed as micro- and macrodimensions of the same task. Faculty and students need to receive specific, comprehensible feedback on the extent to which the teaching and learning process is achieving its desired goals. Just as individual teachers need to make their goals and objectives explicit in order to improve their teaching, so too does a faculty need to make the goals and objectives of the entire curriculum explicit in order to improve student learning.

Since the micro- and macrolevels of classroom assessment and classroom research focus on improving teaching and student learning, both approaches help to keep in front of faculty the distinction between what students are learning and what students should be learning. Classroom assessment has as its agenda the specific questions about student learning that arise within the context of a single faculty member's classroom. Its advantage is that faculty are inclined to act most quickly to make changes when assessment data relate to real student performance or problems in their own classrooms. Collaborative assessment applied to an entire curriculum has as its agenda the specific questions that focus on issues of coherence and integrity of the curriculum and whether students are actually progressing developmentally to meet the expectations established by faculty. The advantage of collaborative assessment is that faculty are cooperating on shared pedagogical concerns, which frequently results in a collegial response to improving the quality of student learning. Such a response recognizes that the process of solving many student learning problems requires a systematic approach across the curriculum rather than selective interventions by an individual faculty member in a single classroom.

Assessment should always be viewed as a means to improve student learning and never as an end in itself. Ideally, assessment is a continuous process concerned with teaching, learning, integrating knowledge and skills, and helping students to become active rather than passive learners. Logically developed methods of assessing student learning in the classroom are valuable because they focus on improving student performance rather than on merely reporting scores to satisfy politicians, bureaucrats, and journalists.

A complete description of the performance-based, course-embedded assessment program developed at King's College to complement its outcomes-oriented curriculum can be found in *Enhancing Student Learning: Emphasizing Essential Competencies in Academic Programs* (Wilkes-Barre, PA: King's College Press, 1988).

In 1993, Donald W. Farmer was vice president for academic affairs, King's College, Wilkes-Barre, Pennsylvania.

———————

Systemwide Assessment of Utah's General Education Courses

Philip I. Kramer

Look for: A faculty-developed approach to statewide assessment of general education outcomes initiated by the Utah State Board of Regents. Following a failed experiment with a national standardized test, faculty groups designed item banks in economics, history, mathematics, and political science. Since faculty were free to choose their own items from the item banks, no institutional comparisons of scores were possible. From Assessment Update *17:2 (2005).*

In 1998, the Utah State Board of Regents ordered a sample administration of American College Testing's Collegiate Assessment of Academic Proficiency (CAAP), a test of general knowledge, for Utah System of Higher Education (USHE) students. The pilot test was administered to 3,148 Utah college students who were completing their sophomore year at one of Utah's nine public colleges or universities.

Although Utah college and university students scored above the national average, the results of the CAAP were considered a disappointment. Faculty throughout the state believed that the CAAP was an inadequate test of general education because (1) the test was not aligned with course content or objectives; (2) the CAAP did not correlate with students' grade point averages; (3) the findings were too general and failed to offer any guidance to faculty; and (4) the CAAP was not administered to students who had taken any specific courses in common or completed similar degree requirements (Utah State Board of Regents, 2000, p. 11). Consequently, the Regents' Task Force for General Education, an ad hoc faculty committee charged by the regents with examining general education in the state, asked the regents to allow faculty members to create their own assessment instruments to measure the general education knowledge of Utah college and university students.

The regents agreed with members of the task force and authorized the group to create and administer course-relevant, content-embedded assessment instruments. However, before assessment instruments were designed, the task force first had to determine the meaning of *general education*. After months of work, the faculty representatives from throughout the state agreed on a set of nine general education competences. This set established the minimum level of knowledge that students were required to attain after completing the second year of general education courses at any of the public institutions of higher education in the state. Nine competences were established in (1) quantitative literacy, (2) writing, (3) social sciences, (4) humanities, (5) life sciences, (6) physical sciences, (7) fine arts, (8) technology and computers, and (9) American institutions.[1]

After agreeing on general education competences, statewide faculty began to develop the pilot assessment. Much of the organization and implementation of the pilot assessment emanated from faculty disciplinary subcommittees. In 2000, a request for proposals had been sent from the task force to the chief academic officers (CAOs) on the nine campuses, inviting the CAOs to participate in the assessment process and to nominate faculty representatives from four disciplines (economics, history, political science, and mathematics) to represent their respective campuses. Over a period of several months, nominated faculty met in small disciplinary groups and developed a bank of course-relevant, content-embedded test questions.

After coming to general agreement about the importance of measuring value-added knowledge, faculty in the disciplinary subcommittees decided to use multiple-choice pretest and posttest questions. Faculty were aware of the limitations of multiple-choice tests; however, creating other types of test questions—for example, essay questions—was not possible due to time and financial constraints.

The mathematics faculty committee refused to use multiple-choice questions. Instead, this committee elected to use a test comprising true-false and fill-in-the-blank questions. Perhaps justifiably differing from the other three disciplines, mathematics faculty insisted on the

---

[1]Successfully completing an American Institutions course is a USHE graduation requirement that students may satisfy by completing either Economics 1740 (U.S. Economic History), History 1700 (American Civilization), or Political Science 1100 (U.S. National Government).

methodological ability to evaluate students' thought processes on the pilot assessment. Thus, students taking the mathematics portion of the pilot assessment test were administered questions on which they were required to show proof of their answers.

A bank of possible test questions was developed for each of the four pretests and posttests. The stated goal was to measure the value added to a student's knowledge base after successfully completing a course in the discipline. Faculty in each discipline at each institution were free to select the test questions from the bank of questions developed for their area by the disciplinary subcommittee. Thus, although all of the disciplinary tests were similar at the different institutions, they were not the same.

The general education pilot assessment was administered to 2,141 students at the nine USHE institutions at the beginning and the end of the spring 2001 semester. Pretest and posttest scores were analyzed from 699 College Algebra (Mathematics 1050) students, 164 U.S. Economic History (Economics 1740) students, 1,207 American Civilization (History 1700) students, and 71 U.S. National Government (Political Science 1100) students. There were dramatic improvements in student learning between the beginning and the end of the semester. Improvement in scores from pretest to posttest ranged from a low of 36 percent in American Civilization to a high of 169 percent in mathematics.

A subsequent study was conducted to examine the purposes of the pilot assessment, how the pilot assessment was organized and implemented, what methodological issues were involved in creating the pilot assessment, and what recommendations participants in the study had for future assessment endeavors. This study used purposeful sampling of participants. In purposeful samples, the participants who are selected have intimate knowledge of the phenomenon being studied. In addition, in this study, participants were chosen who were "considered to be influential, prominent and/or well-informed people," in accordance with guidelines by Marshall and Rossman (1999, p. 113) for designing effective qualitative studies. They were selected as research participants because of their knowledge of and, in some cases, even their expertise in the creation of the pilot assessment that occurred in the spring 2001 semester.

Data collection methods included in-depth interviews of fourteen faculty participants, field note analysis, and analysis of public documents. The analyses of public documents and field notes were used to triangulate the analysis of the participant interviews. Data analysis combined the three separate but concurrent activities of data reduction, data display, and conclusion drawing and verification (Miles and Huberman, 1994). The following highlights characterize the major findings of the study.

Purposes of the General Education Pilot Assessment

The major purposes for the pilot assessment were found to be the following:

- To demonstrate accountability
- To improve teaching and learning
- To compare USHE institutions
- To demonstrate student, faculty, institution, or system performance
- To measure and report the gain in student academic growth
- To articulate or accredit curricula, courses, degrees, or programs for student transfer or matriculation
- To respond to the concern that competence-based assessment conducted at other institutions (for example, Western Governors University) could adversely affect how USHE teaching and learning are measured

Organization and Implementation of Pilot Assessment

The following were identified as major features in organizing and implementing the pilot assessment:

- A standardized, norm-referenced national assessment instrument was rejected by statewide faculty.
- The faculty designed a pilot assessment that was related to the USHE general education curriculum, linked to the curricular goals of the USHE, and embedded in regular course examinations.

- Four faculty disciplinary subcommittees were asked to design the assessment instruments.
- The task force decided to report only aggregated systemwide assessment data because members believed that anonymity would increase participation, and they were concerned that faculty, academic departments, or institutions could be punished for poor assessment results.
- Senior scholars took an active role in the design of the pilot assessment.
- The faculty of the ad hoc Regents' Task Force for General Education and faculty in general took the lead in designing and conducting the pilot assessment.

Methodological Issues of the Pilot Assessment

Some of the major methodological issues included the following:

- Developing a bank of mostly multiple-choice test questions from which individual faculty could select test questions for use in pretests and posttests
- Using course commonalities in the pilot assessment
- Using pretests and posttests in the pilot assessment
- Deciding to embed the pilot assessment posttest in regular final examinations
- Addressing concerns about the possible effect that students' knowledge of pretest results would have on their test-taking ability during the pilot posttest
- Addressing student participation issues in taking the test
- Addressing concerns about test validity and reliability

Recommendations for Future Assessment

Participants were asked to offer recommendations for future general education assessment in the USHE. Participant recommendations included the following:

- Recognize that assessment is important in demonstrating accountability, demonstrating the improvement of teaching and learning, and augmenting institutional accreditation.
- Bring faculty together to communicate about goals, objectives, curriculum, and assessment.
- Provide funding for assessment.
- Clarify assessment goals and objectives.
- Link assessment to faculty development, accountability, and the USHE master plan for higher education.
- Include all stakeholders in the design and implementation of assessment.
- Report assessment results to all stakeholders.

Recommendations for Future Research

Based on the results of this study, the following recommendations for research were made:

- Investigate the effects of the control that various stakeholder groups have in planning, designing, implementing, and reporting on assessment. Specifically, examine how control is exercised and shared and to what extent being in control or having power influences inter-stakeholder relationships and assessment outcomes.
- Examine the issues of stakeholder anonymity and faculty fear of punishment.

Recommendations for Practice

Based on the results of this study, the following recommendations for practitioners were made:

- Although linking accountability with the improvement of teaching and learning has many advantages, the current distrust and misunderstanding among some assessment stakeholders in Utah are such that postponing the link is recommended for the immediate future. Before a link can be established, Utah's assessment stakeholders need to discuss assessment issues, including the responsibility and consequences of teaching and learning; assessment purpose, design, implementation, and reporting; and stakeholder participation and control.

- An assessment advisory board of stakeholder representatives should be created. A major goal of the board should be to guide future assessment efforts in Utah. Specifically, the board would be charged with determining the overall design of an assessment by establishing the purpose of the assessment, appointing individuals and groups to design and implement the assessment, and determining how and to whom the assessment results would be reported. An external consultant would be recruited and hired by the Utah State Board of Regents to serve as an independent analyst of the assessment process and to certify the assessment results.

- Faculty should be in charge of the design of the assessment instrument but not the entire assessment process. Faculty know the curriculum, curricular goals, course content, and how to measure curricular outcomes better than any other stakeholder group. Thus, faculty can best design what is to be measured and how it should be measured.

- Multiple assessment measures should be used. The validity, reliability, and credibility of Utah's systemwide assessment will increase when multiple measures are used. Measures could include multiple-choice examinations, essay examinations, portfolios, faculty-student interviews, and national standardized examinations. A case has been made for using both criterion-referenced and norm-referenced examinations and randomly selecting students from each USHE institution to take them.

- Systemwide assessment should report not only the aggregated system results but also the disaggregated institutional and academic department results. However, before assessment results are disaggregated, the advisory board should address concerns about anonymity, punishment, and faculty resistance. Academic integrity and quality and the need for a transparent system demand that results be reported at several levels.

Acknowledgment

This article is based on my doctoral dissertation, "Planning, Designing, and Conducting Systemwide Assessment in Higher Education: A Case Study of Utah's General Education Pilot Assessment." University of Utah, May 2003, Salt Lake City.

References

Marshall, C., and Rossman, G. B. *Designing Qualitative Research*. (3rd ed.) Thousand Oaks, CA: Sage, 1999.

Miles, M. B., and Huberman, A. M. *Qualitative Data Analysis: An Expanded Sourcebook*. (2nd ed.) Thousand Oaks, CA: Sage, 1994.

Utah State Board of Regents. *Biennial Assessment and Accountability Report*. Salt Lake City: Utah State Board of Regents, 2000.

In 2006, Philip I. Kramer was assistant professor in the Department of Educational Leadership and Foundations and the Department of Teacher Education at the University of Texas at El Paso.

Assessment UPdate
COLLECTIONS

Assessment Update Collections, selected by editor Trudy W. Banta from the rich archives of *Assessment Update*, provide readers with information on specific areas of assessment. The articles represent the best thinking on various topics and are chosen to ensure that readers have relevant, comprehensive information that illustrates effective practice. **Ordering information:** Each booklet costs $14.95 and can be ordered by calling 877.762.2974 or visiting our web site at www.josseybass.com. For bulk discounts, please call Sandy Quade at 203.643.8066.

Assessing Student Learning in the Disciplines Faculty members have developed an array of assessment methods—from comprehensive exams and patient-actors to computer simulations and electronic portfolios—in a variety of major fields. These articles examine disciplinary assessment in political science, psychology, sociology, nursing, teacher education, social work, engineering and technology, business, history, urban studies and planning, communication, and fitness/wellness. 76 pages ISBN 978-0-7879-9572-0

Portfolio Assessment How are portfolios, including Web-based portfolios, used at various institutions to assess and improve programs in general education, the major, advising, and overall institutional effectiveness? These articles describe portfolio scoring methods, students' perspectives on portfolios, how portfolios changed the faculty culture at one college, and more. 80 pages ISBN 0-7879-7286-X

Community College Assessment Nowhere are proven assessment methods needed more than at the community college. These articles illustrate best practices, addressing such issues as evaluating transfer success, assessing employer needs, community and technical college students' perceptions of student engagement, corporate partnerships in assessment, and much more. 80 pages ISBN 0-7879-7287-8

Hallmarks of Effective Outcomes Assessment This booklet illustrates time-tested assessment principles. Useful for those new to assessment as well as experienced practitioners, it details the specific hallmarks required for the success of any assessment program-from leadership and staff development to the assessment of processes as well as outcomes, ongoing communication among constituents, and more. 72 pages ISBN 0-7879-7288-6

About the Editor: Trudy W. Banta is senior advisor to the chancellor for academic planning and evaluation at Indiana University-Purdue University Indianapolis and editor of the bimonthly *Assessment Update: Progress, Trends, and Practices in Higher Education*. Recipient of seven national awards for her work, Banta has directed campuswide assessment programs at the University of Tennessee as well as IUPUI. She has written or edited 14 books and monographs on assessment, including *Building a Scholarship of Assessment* (Jossey-Bass, 2002).